AN AMERICAN LOVE-FEST

KIMBERLY BRATTON

DONALD TRUMP

An American Love-Fest

By
Kimberly Bratton

KIMBERLY BRATTON

Printed in the United States of America
First Printing, 2016
ISBN-13: 978-1530283583
ISBN-10: 1530283582

Vixen Publishing
5280 Haynes Creek Drive
Loganville, GA 30052

Contact Information
Vixen Publishing   www.vixenpublishing.com
Email us at: kimberlybratton@vixenpublishing.com

Head-Shot of Donald J. Trump on the cover was
taken by and is attributed to: Gage Skidmore

DEDICATION

I dedicate this book to the American Patriot, those Americans who hold the values of the Constitution close to heart and consider them inviolate.

Kimberly Bratton

"The stakes of this election are the highest in our lifetimes, in our generation. And everybody needs to be involved in this election. We need to go and compete for the hearts and the minds and the votes of everybody, no matter if we get 2 percent of the vote."

Speaker Paul Ryan

Table of Contents

KIMBERLY BRATTON

DONALD TRUMP

THE RIDE THAT BEGAN IT ALL

On June 16, 2015, the lobby of Trump Tower filled to capacity with cameras and reporters, all vying for a prime location at the base of the iconic escalator.

Located in Midtown Manhattan, Trump Tower is a magnificent edifice. The sixty-eight story building overlooks Central Park and is adorned with luxury at every turn. From its rich wood finishes to burnished gold leaf and bronze mirrors to handcrafted crystal chandeliers, Trump Tower offers those that can afford it, luxury like no other. It's filled with beauty and stepping through the front door is magical, to say the least.

It's like walking into a fantasy world that most of us will never see but the Trump family lives with this beauty every day. The top three floors of Trump Tower are home to the Billionaire Businessman and his beautiful family and are just as spectacular as the hotel itself.

Today, however, Trump Tower is filled with a brilliant energy that extends beyond the glitz and glamour of the decor. That energy seems to grow with each passing moment, as people begin to gather amongst the cameras, waiting also to hear what Donald Trump has to say.

Reporters are primping, while cameramen double-check the equipment, taking no chances that they miss this historic event.

As a contagious excitement spreads quickly through the crowd, reporters contort their bodies into position never thought possible, trying to catch the first glimpse of the man they are here to see, the man emanating the now palpable energy flowing through the room.

Clustered at the base of the escalator, waiting to record the historic event, camera's begin to roll as movement is detected from above.

The people are watching either live on TV or on-line as Donald Trump finally appears at the top of the escalator with his beautiful and elegant wife, Melania Trump.

Standing tall in his blue suit and iconic red tie, he looks at the crowd below and smiles.

Donald Trump has captivated the attention of the entire nation. Some for the first time, and other's like myself, a reunion of sorts.

I've heard about the Trump family my entire life, I've read about his ups and his downs. He's rebuilt his brand many times over and each time he does, he makes it stronger and better than it ever was before. Now where have I heard those words?

America watches in awe as Donald Trump stands with his beautiful wife Melania at the top of the now famous escalator. He waves to his adoring supporters, takes a deep breath and tells her "Honey, let's do this." then he escorts her on for the ride of a lifetime.

It was Ivanka Trump, in a simple white dress, who walked on-stage to greet the swarm of cameras. Without equivocation, she told us all who Donald Trump is to her.

He is a man "who needs no introduction" Ivanka says, as her eyes sparkle and you can almost hear her heart bursting with pride as she speaks to us all on that historic day.

"Welcome everybody. Today I have the honor of introducing a man who needs no introduction. His legend has been built and his accomplishments are too many to name. That man is my father. Most people strive their entire lives to achieve great success in a single field. My father has succeeded in many. At the highest level and on a global scale. He's enjoyed success in a vast diversity of industries because the common denominator is him—his vision, his brilliance, his passion, his work ethic and his refusal to take no for an answer."

"I've enjoyed the good fortune of working alongside my father for 10 years now and I've seen these principles in action daily. I remember him telling me when I was a little girl, 'Ivanka, if you're going to be thinking anyway, you might as well be thinking big.' And that's how he approaches any task that he undertakes. He thinks big. My father has employed tens of thousands of people throughout his career and he has inspired them to do extraordinary things. He has the strength to make hard decisions, and motivate those around him to achieve the impossible. He is an optimist who chases big dreams and sees potential where others do not. He leads by example and will outwork anyone in any room. My father is the opposite of politically correct. He says what he means, and he means what he says."

"He is also the best negotiator I have ever met. Countless times I've stood by his side and watched him make deals that seem to impossible to get done. He has the discernment to understand what the other party means and the commitment to get exactly what he wants. My father knows how to be a fierce opponent, but also how to be a very loyal friend. When it comes to building bridges, he can do so figuratively, but also has the rare ability to do so literally, on time and under budget."

"Throughout his career my father has been repeatedly called upon by local and federal government to step in and save long stalled grossly over budget public projects. Whether it's building a skating rink in the heart of Central Park, meticulously restoring the exterior facade of Grand Central Terminal, enabling the development of New York City's Jacob Javits Convention Center, creating a championship public golf course for the city of New York, or redeveloping the iconic but totally underutilized old post office building on Pennsylvania Avenue and the heart of Washington, D.C., my father succeeds time and time again where government has failed before him."

"I consider myself fortunate to have learned from the best, both as an entrepreneur and as a parent. My father is a man who is deeply grounded in tradition, raised my siblings and me to work hard and to strive for excellence in all that we do. He taught us that we have a responsibility to make a positive contribution to society. Here today, my father is again leading me by example. My generation finds itself at a crossroads. Our leadership has been mired in bureaucracy of its own creation. If we don't adapt politically and economically, our country will be left behind to address the many challenges we face. We don't need talk, we need action, we need execution. We need someone who is bold and independent, with a proven track record of successfully creating and building large and complex and complicated organizations, and in the process enabling many, many Americans to better their lives. I can tell you that there's no better person than my father to have in your corner when you're facing tough opponents or making hard decisions. He is battle tested. He is a dreamer, but perhaps more importantly he is a doer. Ladies and gentlemen, it is my pleasure to introduce to you today a man who I have loved and respected my entire life, my father, Donald Trump".[1]

I have to say, in the past, I never gave much thought to who Ivanka Trump really was. In my mind, growing up in a carefree America, Ivanka Trump was only "the daughter of some rich guy". Today I see a very different person.

I see an accomplished woman who speaks eloquently about the things her father has done and what he can do for America. Ivanka Trump has complete faith in her father and in her words I found that faith, too. She won my heart and before she was finished, I knew that my support was not misplaced.

With our beautiful American Flag displayed proudly behind him, Donald Trump shocked the world. He announced his candidacy for the President of the United States of America.

"We need somebody that literally will take this country and make it great again. We can do that," Trump told the crowd of supporters. "So ladies and gentlemen, I am officially running for President of the United States."

His 45-minute presidential campaign announcement speech included a pledge to restore the "American dream" . . . "Bigger and better and stronger than ever before."

THE MAN

It was New York City that saw the birth of Donald John Trump on June 14, 1946. He's one of five children born to Mary Anne MacLeod and Fred C. Trump.

Donald's father, Fred Trump, was born in Woodhaven, Queens, to German immigrant parents, Elizabeth and Frederick Trump. They emigrated to the United States in 1885. At that time the family surname was Drumpf, but sometime in the 17th century it was changed to Trump.

Donald's mother, Mary Anne, was born in Scotland. At age eighteen, she found herself traveling to the United States. It was there that she met Fred C. Trump and they married in 1936.

The couple had Maryanne in 1937, followed by Fred, Jr. in 1938 and Elizabeth in 1942.

Donald was born next and last but not least, his younger brother, Robert, was born in 1948.

Fred Trump believed in education and discipline and he held each of his children to very high standards.

Donald Trump was given an education to be envious of but it was his hard work and determination to succeed that enabled him to thrive in that environment.

The Fred Trump Family lived in a modest two-story mock-Tudor home on Wareham Place in Jamaica Estates. While living there, Donald attended the private Kew-Forest School,[2] where his father was a member of the Board of Trustees.

In an interview in 1983, Fred stated that Donald was "a pretty rough fellow when he was small", prompting him to enroll Donald in the New York Military Academy (NYMA). Trump attended NYMA from eighth grade through high school.[3]

During his senior year at NYMA, Trump participated in marching drills and while proudly wearing a uniform, Trump earned the rank of "Cadet Captain".[4]

In 2015, he told a biographer that NYMA gave him "more training militarily than a lot of the guys that go into the military".[5]

After leaving NYMA Trump attended Fordham University for two years before entering the Wharton School of Business at the University of Pennsylvania. Wharton showed Donald Trump the world of Real Estate studies and he obviously excelled at their teachings. He graduated in 1968 with a Bachelor of Science degree in Economics.[6]

Some people say that Donald Trump was born with a silver spoon in his mouth and I suppose compared to most of us, that would seem true. People like to say that Donald Trump had it easy after all he inherited everything he has, but that's not entirely true.

When Trump graduated from college, he was worth about $200,000 USD ($1.4 million by 2015 standards).[7] That's certainly more than most of us have when we graduate from college but for Trump it was relatively little compared to his father's actually net worth.

Trump began his real estate career by working alongside his father at his company, Elizabeth Trump and Son, who focused on middle-class rental housing in the boroughs of New York City.

Trump's first project as an under-graduate was a revitalization project involving a foreclosed apartment complex in Cincinnati, Ohio.

Trump's father purchased the complex in 1962 for $5.7 million and after investing only a half-million dollars, they increased the dismal occupancy rate of the 1,200-unit complex from 34% to 100%. In 1972, the Trump Organization sold Swifton Village for $6.75 million dollars.[8]

Trump moved to Manhattan in 1971, involving himself in even grander building projects. Trump's expertise, coupled with his exquisite taste, attracted the attention and recognition of not only his peers but the public as well.

Trumps hotels and golf courses are today known around the world as some of the most luxurious places on earth, with attractive architectural designs and amenities designed to pamper.

In 1973, Trump drew the attention of the public for the first time when he was accused of violating the Fair Housing Act by the United States Justice Department, involving the operation of 39 of his rental properties.

Trump in turn accused the Justice Department of targeting his company because of its size, in an effort to force the property to rent housing to welfare recipients.

Trump settled the charges in 1975, saying he was satisfied that the agreement, which did not "compel the Trump organization to accept persons on welfare as tenants unless as qualified as any other tenant."[9]

I tell that story for one reason only. Donald Trump was 29 years old when the DOJ came after him and he easily won his battle with a department of the government so powerful it has the ability to destroy anyone. Donald Trump beat them at their own game, thus beginning a life of "winning".

Trump wasn't the only sibling to achieve high success. His sister Maryanne Trump Barry was nominated as a Federal District Judge by President Reagan in 1983. She was later appointed by Bill Clinton in 1999 to the United States Court of Appeals for the Third Circuit.

Success, however, didn't befall one of the Trump siblings. In 1981, when Donald was 35, his oldest brother, Fred Trump Jr., tragically died from complications of alcoholism. He was only 42.

I have heard Mr. Trump say, on more than a few occasions, that he has pounded into his children's heads the necessity of abstaining from drugs, alcohol, and even cigarettes.

He doesn't just preach this to his children, he lives this principle himself.

Trump's abstinence from alcohol was largely shaped by the death of his brother, which he explains, "had a tremendous impact" on his life.

"He was a great guy, a handsome person. He was the life of the party. He was a fantastic guy, but he got stuck on alcohol," says Trump, 69. "And it had a profound impact and ultimately [he] became an alcoholic and died of alcoholism. He would tell me, 'Don't drink ever'. He understood the problem that he had and that it was a very hard problem."

"He had a profound impact on my life, because you never know where you're going to end up," Trump adds. "I've known so many people that were so strong and so powerful [yet] they were unable to stop drinking."[10]

Father of five and grandfather to seven, Trump has been consistent in his teachings to his children about the importance of abstaining from drugs and alcohol but he is also a realist. He says "I think they drink a little bit, but not much. But I say no drugs, no alcohol, no cigarettes."

Trump's family has always been the most important thing in his life, however building a multi-billion dollar business takes a lot of time away from the family.

But even though his children might feel like they had an unconventional childhood, they also had one of the most inspiring and motivational father's to look up to and learn from. They knew he was working hard, somewhere, but they also knew, he was only a phone call away.

"I always prided myself on being a good father," he said. "With my children, I was always available."

His daughter Ivanka, 33, agreed: "He was tough, firm, but always available to us."[11]

Donald Trump has spent his entire life buying and selling properties. Some were successful and some were not.

In 1988, Trump acquired the Taj Mahal Casino in a transaction with Merv Griffin and Resorts International. This led to mounting debt, and by 1989, Trump was unable to meet loan payments.

Although he shored up his businesses with additional loans and postponed interest payments, by 1991 the increasing debt forced Trump into business bankruptcy.

Banks and bondholders lost hundreds of millions of dollars but opted to restructure the debt anyway.

The Taj Mahal emerged from bankruptcy on October 5, 1991, with Trump ceding 50 percent ownership in the casino to the original bondholders, in exchange for lower interest rates on the debt and more time to pay it off.

I was a young adult during that time and I remember seeing all this play out on the news. For some reason, I was interested in it, even back then.

Trump was so cash-strapped that he was forced to sell his financially challenged Trump Shuttle airline and his beautiful 282-foot mega-yacht, known as The Trump Princess[12].

I know what you're thinking. It's hard to feel sorry for the millionaire losing his expensive "toys", right?

Trump managed to get back on his feet, but it wasn't until the death of his father in 1999, that he inherited his share of his father's estate. It was reported to be between $250 to $300 million dollar and was divided equally between Donald and his three remaining siblings.[13]

Trump did very well with his inheritance, turning his roughly seventy million dollar inheritance into the multi-billion dollar estate it is today.

In 2015, Forbes estimated Trump's net worth at $4 billion dollars. In June 2015, Business Insider published a 2014 financial statement, supplied by Trump, which reflects his net worth as $8.7 billion.[14]

I would say he's done well with his inheritance, probably better than most would have.

MELANIA TRUMP

Melania Trump was born Melania Knauss on April 26, 1970 in Slovenia. Her parents were Viktor Knavs, who managed a car dealership, and her mother, Amalija, a fashion designer.

Melania grew up in an austere Eastern-block concrete housing unit, living a modest lifestyle, much different than how she lives today.

She began modeling at the age of sixteen and by eighteen years old she had a contract with a modeling agency in Milan.

Not only is she beautiful, but she's also very intelligent. She obtained a degree in Design and Architecture at the University in Slovenia, all the while jetting between photo shoots in Paris and Milan. She's quite impressive, being fluent in five different languages including English, French, Slovenian, Serbian, and German.

The 5 feet 11 inch Slovenian-born brunette, has appeared in numerous fashion magazines and ads and has been photographed by some of the top photographers in the fashion industry.

The below photograph was taken by and is a copyright of Glenn Francis at www.PacificProDigital.com.

Melania is a naturally photogenic beauty and when she steps in front of a camera she owns it. Her captivating presence is seen in every photo they take of her and she has graced the covers of some of the most stylish magazines, including layouts for the Sports Illustrated Swimsuit Issue, Allure, Vogue, Self, Glamour, Vanity Fair, and Elle.

Melania is known world-wide for her modeling but most Americans saw her for the first time on their television sets. She began doing commercials, with her most memorable one being for Aflac, where she stars with that cute little Aflac duck.

Melania displays a natural elegance and grace and her beauty is only surpassed by her devotion to helping others.

She is well known for her charitable contributions to those in need and her generosity can be seen not only in her donations but in her day-to-day work.

She was the Honorary Chairwoman for the Martha Graham Dance Company in April 2005 and the Police Athletic League honored her with their Woman of The Year Award in 2006.

She's been an Honorary Chairwoman for The Boy's Club of New York for five consecutive years, and in 2005 The American Red Cross awarded her with their Goodwill Ambassadorship.

In April of 2008, Melania was asked by NASDAQ and the Love Our Children USA to participate in the Fifth Annual National Love Our Children Day. She was honored by their request that she to kick off the National Child Abuse Prevention month by ringing the closing bell at NASDAQ.

Melania's humanitarian side shines through her philanthropic interests but her kindness can be seen in everything she does.

She's a dedicated New Yorker, having moved to the big city in 1996, where she continued to work diligently, building a highly successful career. It was during that time that she'd meet a man who would change her life forever.

It was September 1998, Fashion Week in New York City and the festivities and parties were in full force.

Trump and Melania were introduced at a party, a full year after his divorce from his second wife, Marla Maples.

He asked for her phone number and she refused. Knowing he was a ladies' man, she didn't want to be one of those women. But before the night was over, Melania Knauss accepted Donald Trump's personal phone number.

She called him a week later and so began an amazing courtship.

They became engaged in 2004, and were married on January 22, 2005 in Palm Beach, Florida.

The wedding was spectacular, attended by some of the most well known people including Heidi Klum, Shaquille O'Neal, Rudy Giuliani, Barbara Walters, Regis Philbin, Kelly Ripa, as well as, then-Senator Hillary Clinton and former President Bill Clinton.

The reception was serenaded by Billy Joel with "Just the Way You Are" and Trump's bride was stunning in a white John Galliano dress, which showed off her beautifully tanned shoulders and graceful neck. Her hair was swept up and her aqua-blue eyes sparkled with love.

The wedding cake weighed in at 50 pounds and was an Orange Grand Marnier chocolate truffle cake, with a Grand Marnier butter-cream icing and filling. It was white, covered with 3,000 white and gold roses and was created by a chef at Mar-A-Lago.

The Trumps' wedding was widely covered by the media, whose appetite for "anything Trump" was insatiable, even back then.

In March of 2006, after settling into her new life, Melania Trump gave birth to a boy, Barron William Trump.

As an infant, Barron reportedly occupied his own floor in the Trump's tri-level apartment in Trump Tower, but like so many parents, the Trumps had their infant son sleep in a crib in their room.

Barron inherited his parent's good genes and intellect, being equally fluent in English and Slovenian, as well as French. It has been reported that he loves to golf with his Dad and likes wearing a suit and tie, prompting Melania to give him the nickname of "Mini-Donald".

Like his older siblings, I'm sure Barron Trump will grow up to be an amazing person, businessman and an asset to his family's business.

Melania and Trump have been near constant companions since their marriage, and are often seen together at New York City society events and receptions.

Barbara Walters, who is well-known for her many talents in the television industry, was so impressed with Melania's intelligence, has said of her: "Maybe because she's so pretty, we don't expect her to be as smart as she is".[15]

In February 2010, Melania Trump followed in her mother's footsteps, launching her own line of jewelry. But she didn't stop there. In March of 2013, Melania added a skin care collection to her already growing business.[16]

Melania Trump has impressed the world in so many ways, from her successful modeling career and lucrative businesses, to standing in front of a massive crowd in Myrtle Beach, South Carolina, as her husband introduces her and Barron to the voters for the first time.

She was already a success even before marrying her billionaire soul mate, but what impresses me most about her right now is her never-ending faith in her husband's ability to "Make America Great Again".[17]

It is Melania Trump who stands behind the man that we have all come to admire.

I do believe that had Melania Trump not thrown herself completely behind her husband, he would not be running today. I have watched interviews and read articles of the two of them together and what I see is a completely compatible couple, comfortable not only with each other but in their own skins as well.

Thank you Melania, for giving your husband of more than a decade, the encouragement and support needed for him to accomplish his goals. I want to also thank you and the rest of the Trump Family, on behalf of his many loyal supporters, for your selflessness in sharing such a brilliant and hard working man with the rejuvenated and hopeful American public.

THE TRUMP CHILDREN

Donald Trump's 1977 marriage to the Czechoslovakian model, Ivana Trump, produced his first three children and heirs to the Trump fortune.

Donald John "Don" Trump, Jr. was born in Manhattan, on December 31, 1977. Today he is a successful businessman working along his sister Ivanka Trump and brother Eric Trump. Donald Trump Jr. currently holds the title of Executive Vice President of The Trump Organization.

Ivanka Marie Trump, born in Manhattan on October 30, 1981, inherited her beauty from her mother, Ivana, and her business-sense from her father, Donald Trump.

Ivanka Trump is a formal model, a writer and a successful businesswoman. In her role as Executive Vice President of Development & Acquisitions at the Trump Organization, she is involved in all aspects of the company's real estate and hotel management initiatives.

When asked about her drive and that of her siblings, she stated rather succinctly, "I look at my brothers and myself and I'm, like, really proud of the fact that nobody's, like, totally f**ked-up. Nobody's a drug addict, nobody's driving around chasing women, snorting coke."[18]

She's the principal owner of Ivanka Trump Fine Jewelry and the Ivanka Trump Lifestyle Collection which includes fragrances, footwear, handbags, outerwear and an eye-wear collection.

Like her siblings, her education is beyond reproach. Ivanka attended the Chapin School in New York until age 15, then transferred to and graduated from Choate Rosemary Hall in Wallingford, Connecticut.

She spent two years at Georgetown University, then transferred to the Wharton School at the University of Pennsylvania (her father's alma mater), graduating cum laude in 2004 with a B.S. in Economics.[19]

Eric Frederic Trump was born on January 6, 1984. He is a successful businessman and philanthropist. As the Executive Vice President of Development and Acquisitions at The Trump Organization, he directs all new project acquisitions and development throughout the world alongside his brother, Donald, Jr., and sister, Ivanka. In 2006, he founded The Eric Trump Foundation, which has pledged and donated over $28 million to St. Jude Children's Research Hospital.[20] He also owns Trump Winery.[21]

Their mother, Ivana Trump isn't just a pretty face, she's smart too. She would eventually take a major role in the Trump Organization, becoming the Vice President of Interior Design. Ivana Trump is credited for creating the signature designs of the Trump Tower which prompted Trump to appoint his wife to head up the Trump Castle Hotel and Casino as president. The Czech-born wife of Donald Trump and successful by her own rights, became a naturalized U.S. citizen in 1988, with Donald Trump at her side.[22]

In the late 1980's, Mrs. Trump wanted to leave the business world to devote more time to her family. However, her husband asked her to oversee the restoration of the landmark Plaza Hotel, so instead of leaving, she took over as its president.

In 1990, Ivana was named Hotelier of the Year, making her a legend within the Trump Organization. Life was pretty good for her and her family. They lived a charmed life with the security of wealth that most of us can't begin to fathom. But as they say "money doesn't buy happiness" and Ivana Trump would soon realize that truth.

Towards the end of 1990, Ivana became aware of rumors circulating that her husband, Donald, was having an affair with a former beauty queen from Georgia, Marla Maples.

While on a family Christmas holiday in Aspen, Ivana encountered Marla Maples on the ski slopes; their ugly confrontation was reported in the New York Post the following day.

After suffering tremendous humiliation, Ivana retained entertainment attorney Neil Papiano and filed for divorce. That was 1991.

The often-times ugly divorce proceedings were splashed all across the tabloids. They were like bloodsuckers, in their efforts to be the first to report the details as scandalously as possible. The Trump divorce was finally settled in 1992,[23] Ivanka Trump was ten years old at the time.

Her father later married his mistress, Marla Maples, who gave birth to Tiffany, the Trump children's half-sister.

Donald and Marla didn't last very long, divorcing when Tiffany was five, at which time Marla moved her beautiful young daughter to California. Tiffany wasn't a huge part of the Trump family dynamics and has stayed out of the spotlight for most of her life. But the 22-year-old blond beauty finally stepped up, by appearing alongside her half-siblings on ABC's "20/20" with Barbara Walters, to talk about their famous father.[24]

Even though the Trump siblings didn't spend a lot of time together in their youth, it seems to me, after watching the Barbara Walters interview, that they are very close as adults.

I saw four amazing adult children, all standing together in support of their father. But more than that, I saw patriots, who love this country, and like their father, they want to see us, the American people achieve the American Dream.

The Trump children, without hesitation, are willing to share their wonderful, accomplished father with all of us.

TRUMP POLITICAL HISTORY

For decades, there's been talk of a potential presidential run for Donald Trump. In nearly every election, I'd hear rumors immediately begin to circulate, although I never really gave the idea much merit. But by 2008, I really wanted to see him run.

Donald Trump was busy building a successful company, and like the rest of us, he entrusted the politicians to get the job done.

But year after year the politicians kept digging our country into a giant hole. In October 1999, Trump had had enough and declared himself a presidential candidate for the The Reform Party of the USA(RPUSA), generally known the Reform Party, founded in 1995 by Ross Perot. On February 14, 2000, Donald Trump withdrew his bid and support for the Reform Party.[25] And by 2004, Donald Trump identified himself as a Democrat, openly supporting Hillary Clinton, and donating large sums of money to Democratic groups.[26]

After deciding that the Democrats no longer shared his beliefs, Trump changed parties again, this time registering as a Republican in 2009.

By early 2011, speculation of a Trump presidential run was once again reaching full crescendo. Trump began to take the lead in polls among Republican candidates in the 2012 election cycle, in spite of the fact that he wasn't even running.

In 2011, polls showed Trump to be among the leading candidates. A Wall Street Journal/NBC News poll from March 2011 showed Trump in the lead for the Republican nomination for president of the United States.[27]

A February 2011 Newsweek poll placed Trump within a few points of President Obama in a potential 2012 presidential contest, with many voters still undecided.[28]A poll released in April 2011 by Public Policy Polling showed Trump having a nine-point lead in a potential contest for the Republican nomination while still only considering a run.[29]

In December 2011, Trump placed sixth in the "ten most admired men and women living of 2011" according to the USA Today/Gallup telephone survey.[30]

There was so much speculation as to his run, Donald Trump was forced to officially announce in May 2011 that he would not be running for the office.[31] Many people were disappointed, myself included.

At the 2011 *Conservative Political Action Conference*(CPAC), Trump said he is "pro-life" and "against gun control". In late 2008, Trump was a supporter of the 2009 government backed rescue plan for the U.S. auto industry which by 2012 gained the support of 56% of Americans, according to a Pew Research Center poll.[32]

In 2013, Trump began researching the possibilities of a 2016 run for President of the United States.[33]

In February 2015, Trump decided not to renew his television contract for *The Apprentice*, which again fueled speculation of a potential Trump run.[34]

In May 2015, Trump said he was opposed to granting President Barack Obama fast track trade authority in the *Trans-Pacific Partnership*. Instead, Trump expressed a desire for stronger negotiations with China on trade, coupled with tariffs, if necessary.[35]

Trump is a business man, not a politician. But he's been a part of the political world for most of his adult life. He's donated to both sides and he's seen the back room deals. He knows how it all works and that's exactly what we need right now.

We've been lied to and manipulated by career politicians and most of the time, we are kept completely in the dark. Donald Trump has shined a spot-light into the dark corners revealing the ugliness of our political system. He has exposed the corruption between the politicians and the media that we all suspected was taking place, but could never really prove.

It took a man as powerful and as brave as Donald Trump to speak to the evil of political correctness, freeing us from its strangling grip on our nation. It simple took Donald Trump to say the words that were on all of our tongues and for the first time in a long time, we can all speak the truth without fear.

Regardless of his political past, today Donald Trump has given Americans the strength and the courage to fight this time and for many Americans, they sincerely believe that Donald Trump is their one final hope for a better tomorrow.

AN UNLIKELY SOURCE

I'm a political junkie, have been for years and while watching the news and reading articles and comments, I became aware of what looked like a building fascination on the part of some Americans for Donald Trump. I know I was fascinated with him.

From the minute Donald Trump announced his run, I became a loyal supporter. My family and friends knew this fact about me from the post on my Facebook page and some of them were not all that happy about it. I came face to face with that displeasure one day from an unlikely source.

My soldier son was on leave, coming home for the holidays, so my husband and I drove to the airport to pick him up.

We were early and had to circle the airport fourteen times but when it was close to time for him to arrive, Greg dropped me off at the front door and I ran inside to find my long last pup. I just couldn't wait to get my hands on him and kiss all over his face, a face I am sure now belongs to a man. He's only been away for seven months but it seems like a lifetime to me.

I circled baggage claim looking for my soldier, when all of the sudden, he came up behind me and said "Hey Mom" and those were the sweetest words I'd ever heard.

I turned and grabbed my son, who was now a man, and we hugged each other like we'd been apart for decades. I kissed all over his face and we headed to the car.

His father met us outside and my son offered his dad an outstretched hand, a real man's handshake. I giggled inside but I felt such pride. Then my husband grabbed his son and gave him a big hug, father to son. It was so wonderful to have him home. I was ecstatic but it didn't last long.

On the ride home, after chattering for a few minutes, my son hit me with something quite unexpected, He asked his mother, the known conservative political junkie, this surprising question; "Mom, how can you support Donald Trump?"

I took a deep breath because this was not a conversation I was prepared to have. I was so happy to see my son and the warmth of the hug I got from him standing in the airport terminal was only just beginning to fade away. Couldn't we have just a bit more time to enjoy his homecoming before we got into politics?

So I told my 19 year old son as much, but he insisted with "No, Mom, I really want to know".

We then got into such a deep back and forth that even my husband, the driver, was paying more attention to us then he was in looking for our exit. We went several exits past before we caught our mistake, our second mistake.

The first mistake was having this conversation in the first place, because in it, I found out something horrifying about my son. He's a Bernie Sanders supporter, or so he thinks.

It was that conversation with my son that showed me the full extent of the bias against Mr. Trump. My son has never been around anyone but me, so in my mind, he should think like me. I was dismayed to find out that he doesn't. This was an affront to me and my husband's conservative sensibilities and I couldn't have that.

In talking to my son, I realized that the things he thought he knew about Donald Trump were really only false talking points he'd gotten from the liberal leaning websites he frequents.

I've never made any secret in my home where I stood politically and my children knew that I was a Republican. However, my son seemed to have adopted a different ideology at some point.

I thought "If that's what the son of a very politically savvy, conservative woman thinks, then there must be so many who think the same way he does".

So I decided on the material for the book. I was going to find out myself what people really thought of Donald Trump. I wanted to know who his supporters were and why they supported the Anti-establishment candidate.

I set up a website, one that didn't cost a million dollars that never worked, but one for supporters of Trump, who want their words to be heard. I prepared a political survey to be filled out and submitted back to me and I was surprised to see how willing Americans were to tell me what how they really felt.

During the last six weeks, I received so many replies and the information I gathered was interesting to say the least. I knew how I felt about Mr. Trump but was thrilled to find out so many others felt the same way I did and why.

As I continued to read their answers, I come away thinking that no one really understood the scope of the growing support out there for Donald Trump.

I was shocked to discover that Trump was actually tapping into a large segment of not only the Republican base but also the base of the Democrat party.

I discovered that Trump supporters were not just the lunatic fringe or angry people looking to join a trendy movement, as the media would like you to think. But they actually come from a diverse background, ethnicity and ideology. They are like you and me and they all seem to want the same things.

I am fiscally conservative and pro-life although I value the right of the woman to make her own choices. I sit on the fence on most social issues, so you see, it is possible to see both sides of an issue.

I truly love this country and the people in it but in my opinion, our country is heading in the wrong direction and is in deep trouble.

My concerns for the country are primarily the same as everyone else's, regardless of political party.

The Americans I surveyed are concerned about the debt, the economy, radical Islamic terrorism, illegal immigration, and reforming the tax code so that all Americans pay at least something in taxes.

They want social security protected and they want entitlement and welfare programs revamped so that fraud and abuse is removed. They want their religious freedoms guaranteed once again and they support strengthening of our military and providing proper care to our soldiers and vets.

They want our wounded warriors treated better than the illegal immigrants that the Obama administration cherishes so dearly. They want illegal immigration stopped and they want to feel safe in their own country again.

Neither side will seriously address any of these issues, all the while assuring us with their meaningless rhetoric.

One of the things I personally find most disturbing about our current political class is the seemingly polar opposites that they appear to be but really aren't.

They battle it out on the chamber floor, but once the camera's are off, they are high-fiving each other as they sling back beers at the local pub. They put on a great dog and pony show for us, the American People, but really, they have each other's backs and not ours.

I'm a writer, an IT Technician, a certified cake decorator and I have a family that I adore.

My husband and I own a beautiful home on a five acre piece of land in the country. I raise chickens for their eggs and affection; my life is quite simple and pleasing.

My husband has terminal cancer but we deal with that every day. I don't have a lot of worries, like most of the population, but what keeps me up at night is my grandson, Dexter. I worry so much about what his life is going to be like. I want more than anything for him to grow up in a carefree America, like I did, but that's not going to happen and that makes me angry.

The elephant in the room, the reason for America's decline is rooted primarily in Political Correctness.

It seems insane that something so seemingly trivial has had the ability to bring our country to a grinding halt, but it has.

Political correctness is a cancer on our everyday lives because the sensitivity to it is counter-productive to many of our core beliefs. Beliefs this country was founded on.

When our country is no longer allowed to build structures or even repair current infrastructure because there is some frog, or beetle, or even a tiny flower found nearby which causes years of delay trying to obtain a sometimes impossible to get, environmental impact statements, then we have a serious problem.

The surveys I received from across the country gave a clear understanding of Donald Trump's unexpected rise. Broadly speaking, the men and women who so bravely responded, fall into two basic categories:

1. Those who truly believe that Trump is the best choice to lead America and,

2. Those who want to believe but are afraid he is just going to be another politician.

Of course, any front-runner of a major party is going to have supporters from different backgrounds and world views, but several recurring themes kept appearing and it became clear that most people either loved Trump or they didn't. But the ones who loved him, all felt strongly and were seemingly loyal to the end. Only time will tell.

TRUMP DOMINATES THE INTERNET

With the technology available today, Google did a study to determine which candidate was dominating the on-line searches. The study took place in the month after Donald Trump announced his bid for the office.

Google was hoping to measure just how popular Donald Trump really was versus the other candidates, particularly among those identifying themselves as conservative Republicans in the country.

In August of 2015, Google Trends released the map below which shows searches by candidate. The candidates by color is a little hard to make out below but it goes like this:[36]

CANDIDATES	COLOR
BUSH	GREEN
CARSON	WHITE
CRUZ	ORANGE
JINDAL	BLUE

PAUL   LT VIOLET
TRUMP   RED
WALKER   PEACH
OTHERS   LT PINK

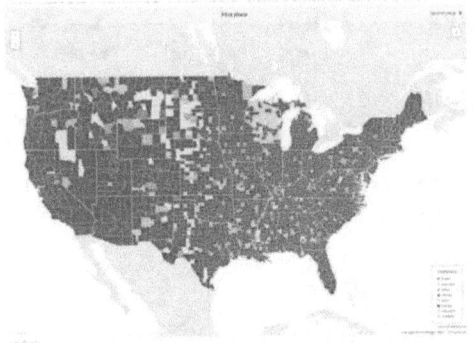

We can see above a county-by-county map of all on-line searches for the Republican candidates, and it's quite clear that Donald Trump, represented in red, blew his competitors away.

Twitter is another was to verify the ever-growing support behind Donald Trump. If you take a look at the increase in followers since October, you can see a steady rise in his support.

Rate of increase in Twitter Followers from October 2015 on.

10/20	4,630,000	
10/21	4,634,000	+4000
10/22	4,640,000	+6000
10/23	4,650,000	+10,000
10/27	4,678,000	+28,000
10/28	4,683,000	+5000
11/07	4,751,000	+68,000

11/08	4,781,000	+10,000
11/11	4,803,000	+22,000
11/14	4,855,000	+52,000
11/16	4,893,000	+38,000
11/18	4,926,000	+33,000
11/21	4,956,000	+40,000
11/25	5,004,000	+48,000
11/27	5,020,000	+16,000
11/30	5,038,000	+18,000
12/28	5,468,000	+430,000
12/30	5,500,000	+32,000
01/04	5,536,000	+36,000
01/07	5,575,000	+39,000
02/18	6,200,000	+625,000

On Facebook, Donald Trump currently has 5,782,000 people hanging on his every word.

He uses Social Media with the same brilliance as Barack Obama, realizing that in today's world, you have to be tech savvy or you perish. Donald Trump is growing more popular with every passing day.

ENDORSEMENTS

WHY THEY MATTER

Political candidates can often increase their name recognition and credibility with the voters by winning celebrity endorsements.

While it is debatable whether or not endorsements will translate into actual votes, some endorsements can be quite beneficial to the candidate.

They play a very important role in the election process and in presidential primaries, endorsements have been among the best predictors of which candidates might succeed and which will not.

An endorsement is when someone with credibility vouches for a certain candidate, service, and or product.

The right endorsement is an extremely effective means of providing a potential voter with the logic and the security to make a positive decision.

In the political world, an positive endorsements will usually illicit positive media attention for a candidate, thereby increasing the poll numbers of the candidate.

These increases generate more media coverage, which in turn generates more endorsements, eventually weeding out most of the competition.

But whether those endorsements affect voter outcome depends on how voters were leaning in the first place.

Kurt Corbello of Southeastern Louisiana University's political science department says this, "Endorsements have three different audiences of potential benefit to the campaign: voters, volunteers, and financial contributors. I think that endorsements are more so a tool to attract money and volunteers, in the hopes that voters will follow, although their added benefit may be in some capability to sway last-minute, undecided voters in a close election," Corbello said.

Pearson Cross, political science professor at the University of Louisiana at Lafayette says, "Data doesn't suggest that endorsements move too many votes. Still, candidates love to be endorsed by people who support their principles."

"Endorsements are important," said Joshua Stockley, political science professor at the University of Louisiana in Monroe, "If endorsements weren't important, politicians would have ceased seeking them decades ago."

However, the gentlemen agree that endorsements do have an impact on elections, but not in the way you might think.

"An endorsement is not going to change someone's mind if the voter was inclined to vote for one candidate over another", Stockley said. "They only serve to legitimize how people are already leaning."

The best example is known in political science circles as "The O Effect" when Oprah Winfrey endorsed President Barack Obama. "It legitimized how people were already feeling," he said. "It made them feel better about voting for him."[37]

Of course, an election can be won without a single endorsement, but in a tight race, the financial and organizational benefits that come with one can make all the difference in the world.

In researching endorsements for Donald Trump, I was amazed not only by the sheer number of them, but in some case, I was very surprised by who they were.

I have compiled a list but Trumps endorsements are coming faster than I can type, so I hope I haven't left anyone off, but if I have, it wasn't intentional. Please enjoy reading each of them. I know I did.

POLITICAL AND BUSINESS ENDORSEMENTS

Donald Trump has received the endorsement of so many from politicians to celebrities. His appeal is broad and his supporters are diverse.

As of the last week of January 2016, a mere days before the Iowa caucus takes place, the first in the country, the list of endorsements for Donald Trump is as follows:

Governor Scott Brown endorses Donald Trump because he's an agent for change, someone who will end the gridlock in Washington. "He's a business man who surrounds himself by brilliant people with new and innovative ideas, all the things he's been saying are true and need to be talked about and dealt with." Brown says, "Whether you agree with Trump's choice of words, he is right in the things he says and he's not afraid to say them.[38]"

Virgil Goode of Virginia, the former U.S. Representative who was also the Constitutional Party presidential nominee in 2012.[39]

Jeff Lord, former White House Associate Political Director for the Reagan administration (1987–88).[40]

Jeff DeWit, State Treasurer of Arizona[41], *Bob Corbin*, former Arizona Attorney General[42] and *Carol Springer*, former State Treasurer of Arizona[43] and *Henry McMaster*, Lieutenant Governor of South Carolina.

Three former Arizona State Senators: *Lori Klein*, *Robert Blendu*, and *Thayer Verschoor* also endorsed.

Two Alabama State Representatives: *Ed Henry*[44] and *Jim Carns*[45], along with my Georgia State Senators: *Burt Jones*[46] and *Michael Williams*.

Iowa State Senator: *Brad Zaun*[47]

Former Louisiana State Representative *Stephen L. Gunn*,[48] an Independent and Former New Hampshire State Senator *Richard Ferdinando*[49] and *Nevada State Assemblyman Brent Jones*.

Nine New Hampshire State Representatives have also endorsed. Those include, *Jenn Coffey*(former),[50] *Fred Doucette*,[51] *Lou Gargiulo*[52] (former), *Werner Horn, Paula Johnson*(former),[53] *Joe Pitre*,[54] Deputy Majority Leader, *Stephen Stepanek*,[55] *Dan Tamburello*,[56] *Robert Fisher* and *Joshua Whitehouse*.[57]

New Jersey State Senator, *Michael J. Doherty*,[58] two Oklahoma State Senators: *Ralph Shortey* and *Mark Allen* and three Oklahoma State Representatives: *Mike Christian, John R. Bennett, Mike Turner*[59](former) and Rhode Island State Representative, *Joseph A. Trillo*[60] have all thrown their support behind Donald Trump.

South Carolina State Senator *John Russell* (former, also former representative, and son of former

Democratic Governor Donald S. Russell) and Jake Knotts.[61]

South Carolina State Representative *James H. Merrill* (also former Majority Leader).[62]

West Virginia State Senator: *Mark R. Maynard* and five West Virginia State Delegates, including *Randy Smith, Ron Walters, Brad White, Ray Canterbury,* and *Joshua Nelson.*[63]

In addition to the politicians giving Trump their support, some of the leading business people are also proud to endorse Trump for President. They include:

Adrie Groeneweg, co-founder of Pizza Ranch chain of restaurants.[64]

Carl Icahn, billionaire activist investor.[65]

Robert Kiyosaki, businessman and author who authored two business books with the candidate.[66]

Charles Kushner, real estate developer and co-owner of Kushner Properties and *Jared Kushner,* co-owner of Kushner Properties, owner of The New York Observer, son-in-law of the candidate.[67]

Nancy Mace, businesswoman and author[68] and *Willie Robertson,* CEO of Duck Commander, and the star of Duck Dynasty[69] who previously endorsed Bobby Jindal until Jindal dropped out of the race.

Phil Ruffin,[70] businessman and partner of Trump Hotel Las Vegas and *Ivanka Trump,* businesswoman, writer, former model and daughter of Donald Trump[71] and *Dana White,* president of Ultimate Fighting Championship.[72]

International political figures include *Matteo Salvini,* Italian MEP and leader of Lega Nord.[73]

Vojislav Šešelj, former Deputy Prime Minister of Serbia[74] and *Geert Wilders,* Dutch MP and leader of the Party for Freedom.[75]

Organizational endorsements include:

American Freedom Party[76], the *National Black Republican Association*[77] and the *New England Police Benevolent Association* [78]have all given Donald Trump their support. The Rent Is Too Dam High Party endorsed Donald Trump also.[79]

These were boring, yes, but now we come to the good stuff.

THE DUKE AND A LEGEND

It's January 19, 2016 and it's frigid here in Atlanta but not nearly as cold as it is in Winterset, Iowa, where a small, intimate gathering has formed at the John Wayne Museum.

On January 17, 2016, Trump's Facebook followers received a very interesting status update from Mr. Trump.

It said, "Join me on Tuesday, January 19th at the Iowa State University, Hansen Agricultural Student Learning Center in Ames, Iowa! I will have a major announcement and a very special guest in attendance. You will not want to miss this rally![80]"

We are all waiting anxiously to see what the announcement is. We know it's an endorsement but by whom?

I'm watching the event via Right Side Broadcasting on You Tube[81] and right now there are thousands tuned in.

The podium is placed in front of a typical western prairie with blue skies, a saddle hangs across the fence and John Wayne stand proudly nearby. Two alpha males, one a legend and one who is going to save our country. John Wayne would be proud.

Aissa Wayne, the daughter of America's hero John Wayne, introduced Donald Trump as "a legend in the making", as she warmly extends her endorsement and the endorsement of the John Wayne Museum behind Donald Trump for President.[82]

Receiving the endorsement of the museum is major in and of itself but that's not the huge announcement scheduled for today. To the dismay of many, Trump informs us all that we'll have to wait until his third rally, which is later tonight to find out who this mystery endorsement is.

So I watched the first and the second and before we got to the third rally, the announcement was leaked to the press, confirmed by Donald Trump's campaign and heads began to explode all over the country within seconds.

There is only one person right now that Liberals hate more than Donald Trump and that is former Alaska Governor Sarah Palin.

They have hated her from the minute she appeared on stage with John McCain where she gave a rousing speech that rejuvenated a nearly comatose McCain Campaign.

But all it ever takes is the mere mention of her name and it's "Liberals Lose Their Mind" hour, displayed for all to see.

I was in front of my television in 2008, watching, as was the rest of the country, when John McCain announced his running mate. She was someone I wasn't familiar with and when I saw her walk on stage, I thought "She's too pretty to be smart." Yes, I'm ashamed to say, that was my first thought and then she opened her mouth to speak.

I was already a McCain supporter in 2008 but I was losing hope fast that John McCain could beat the newly arrived, virtually unknown, junior Senator and community organizer from Chicago, who was taking the country by storm.

This seemingly "nobody" popped his head onto the stage, catching Hillary Clinton off guard and easily beating her to a pulp in the primaries of 2008. This charismatic man, whom none of us had ever heard of, stepped in and stole the Democrat nomination from their "inevitable" queen.

Boy was she mad and I was scared. If he could do that to Hillary Clinton, then John McCain would be a walk-in-the-park for him. All hope was gone, then Sarah Palin takes the stage.

I was drawn in immediately as Sarah spoke passionately to a Convention Hall full of people. She seemed a tad nervous at first, as was I, because I wasn't sure how this "pretty woman" was going to pull this off.

After a few minutes, I began to relax. She was speaking from her heart in that folksy way she has and the audience loved her. She spoke to the moms of the country, endearing herself to women just like me with her joke of "What's the difference between a hockey mom and a pit-bull?. Lipstick." We loved it and it seemed to me that Sarah Palin was "just one of us".

By the time she was finished, she'd won me over. Here was a woman who seemed unafraid, strong and capable of doing anything she set her mind to. I saw someone who just might be able to breathe new life into a dying John McCain. For the first time, hope began to resurface inside of me that this woman could save the day.

Like so many other people, I fell in love with Sarah Palin during that speech. And then the biased media began their unrelenting crusade to take her down and they did.

Sarah Palin is an American politician, former Fox commentator, and author who served as the ninth Governor of Alaska from 2006 to her resignation in 2009.

Sarah Palin is an amazing woman and her record of endorsements is unbelievable. A perfect example is the 2012 Ted Cruz campaign for the seat of vacating U.S. Senator from Texas, Kay Bailey Hutchison.

Cruz's campaign was floundering and his poll numbers remained in the single digits, even though he was running as a True Conservative. It wasn't until Sarah Palin endorsed Cruz that he was able to capture the vote of most all conservatives and eventually win his Senate seat.[83]

Almost every candidate fortunate enough to receive a Palin endorsement has gone on to win, sometimes with quite large margins.

Her influence over American politics is undeniable and that's the reason the Liberal Left, as well as the media, hate her so vehemently.

In 2008, immediately after John McCain introduced Palin to the world, the biased Mainstream Media began an orchestrated attack, not only on Sarah Palin, but her family as well. They dragged her family through the mud, even her newborn baby son, born with Down Syndrome.

The attacks on her character and intelligence were despicable but they were beginning to work.

Then came along Tina Fey's infamous Saturday Night Live skit, in which she portrayed a very dumb Sarah Palin.[84] Fey was effective and so proud of herself for "taking down" a Republican Vice Presidential candidate with something as mundane as a SNL skit.

Never before, at least not in my lifetime, have I heard of a candidate so viciously attacked and systematically destroyed by a collaborative and biased media, as was the case for Vice Presidential Candidate Sarah Palin.

They were nasty and deliberate in their efforts to tear her to pieces and John McCain, well, he "muzzled" his VP choice. She wasn't allowed to defend herself against these attacks nor was she allowed to bring up any issues against Barack Obama. McCain wanted to "play it safe" with absolute political correctness and as I watched, the once vibrant and passionate Sarah Palin began to fade.

Barack Obama went on to easily defeat McCain and Palin in 2008, becoming the First African American U.S. President.

With Donald Trump receiving the coveted Palin endorsement, the media is at it again, only this time she will fight back. They have done all they can do to her and her family and she's still standing and she's still fighting. She is now on the side of a true Alpha Male, one who will never let political correctness get in the way of "winning", one who will never tell her to "shut up and sit down." Thank you, Sarah Palin, you make us women proud.

Trump didn't in any way "need" a Palin endorsement, but it sure makes me smile that Sarah

Palin chose Donald Trump over her once favored Ted Cruz for President of the United States of America.

Avatar: Perplexed:
"You don't get a better endorsement than Sarah Palin! Now I'm certain that I am backing the right candidate. Trump 2016!"

Avatar: Male Man:
"The job is to win Iowa.....Sarah GOD Bless her soul will help Trump do just that......Trump is a fine man and Sarah a good person and the only reason McCain had any chance....But McCain even screwed that up........After the Iowa win Trump will not have to look back......Good.....Trump 2016"

Avatar: John Doe:
"And that, ladies and gentlemen, is how you become the next President of the United States!!"

Avatar: ****Nothing Makes Sense****:
"WOW just WOW. TRUMP WILL MAKE AMERICA GREAT AGAIN!!!"

Avatar: Southern Yankee:
"Sarah gave one hell of a speech, and she hit everyone of my hot button issues, just like Trump does, he will win in a landslide."

CELEBRITY ENDORSEMENTS

Only in recent election cycles, really only since the election of Barack Obama, have celebrities been so willing to stand behind a certain candidate. Even to their detriment at times. Take the Dixie Chicks for example. Does anyone remember who they are?

The Dixie Chicks were three beautiful and talented women who were loved worldwide and put on a terrific show. Twelve years ago, in 2003, Natalie Maines, lead singer of the Dixie Chicks stood in front of a crowd at Shepherd's Bush Empire Theater in England, and uttered these now infamous words:

"Just so you know, we're on the good side with y'all. We do not want this war, this violence, and we're ashamed that the President of the United States is from Texas."

Natalie's comments were made at one of their first stops on a world tour and unfortunately for the Dixie Chicks, the comments sparked off possibly the biggest and most successful "black balling" in the history of American music.

Those horrible words spoken by Natalie Maine, just 10 days before the beginning of the Iraq War, sent the promising careers of the Dixie Chicks into the toilet. They went from being the biggest concert draw in the country music industry to relative obscurity in a matter of weeks.

Despite numerous apologies from Natalie Maines and the Dixie Chicks, a full on boycott of their music was already underway. It was called for and implemented by Americans who love their country and whether you agreed with Bush or not, Natalie's words, made on foreign soil, angered most all of us.

Those flippant words cost the talented women hugely as their new hit "Landslide" went from #10 on the Billboard charts to #44 in only 1 week, falling off the charts completely within another week.

The retaliation from most Americans didn't stop there. Radio stations who played any Dixie Chicks songs were immediately bombarded with phone calls and emails blasting the station and threatening boycotts if they continued.

Even DJ's who sympathized with the Dixie Chicks were forced to stop playing them because of the backlash from their listeners. Some DJ's were even fired when they refused to honor the boycotts demanded by Americans.[85]

Dixie Chicks CD's were rounded up, and in one famous incident, supposedly run over by a bulldozer. Concerts were canceled in the US as the Dixie Chicks couldn't sell tickets, and the Dixie Chicks lost a major sponsor, Lipton.

Another blow came when The Red Cross denied a million dollar endorsement from the band, fearing it would draw the ire of the boycott. The Dixie Chicks also received death threats because of Maines' regrettable words spoken in London.

They pretty much disappeared from the scene in 2008, in spite of their 2006 album, *Taking The Long Way,* debuting at #1 on the Billboard country charts with virtually no radio play.[86] The new album was intended to rejuvenate their careers and even though it went gold in its first week, the anticipated rejuvenation never really happened.

The Dixie Chicks learned the hard way about mixing business and politics and because of what happened to them, other celebrities learned to keep their mouths shut. After all, we pay them to entertain us, not for their political opinions.

The candidacy of Barack Obama changed that as Hollywood whole-heartedly threw its support behind the junior Senator from Chicago, who was running for the highest office of the land and they succeeded.

Today Hollywood is trying once again to affect the outcome of an election as they did for Barack Obama. This time however, they aren't pulling together to support a certain candidate. They are pulling together to make sure that the People's Choice for President doesn't make it to the finish line. They want another Democrat and they'll stop at nothing to make sure that they get one.

There are some brave people still out there, celebrities we all know and love, who are willing to stand up for a man they all know through the industry, but also for the candidate that they believe, as we all do, will save America from the "fundamental transformation" that President Obama has been so successful in implementing.

We all love to read about the endorsements of mega-powers for our candidates so I want to personally thank those brave individuals for not being afraid of political correctness and the bullishness of their fellow actors and entertainers.

Wayne Newton, "Mr. Las Vegas," who's like so many others have predicted that President Obama will go down in history as the worst president ever. He gave Trump his support on a Fox and Friends episode in October of 2015.[87]

Mr. Newton told Fox and Friends, "I love Donald, and he would make a great president, for many reasons," Newton said. "Number one: he tells the truth. Number two: he's been where most of these guys want to be, in terms of riding on his own plane. He doesn't have to worry about what hotels he stays in, doesn't have to worry about how his family gets to Hawaii.... I could give you so many reasons, but most of all, most important for Mr. Trump is: he tells it like it is."

Loretta Lynn, Country Music Legend, whose life story was portrayed by Sissy Spacek in the hit movie *Coal Miner's Daughter*, is a huge fan of Donald Trump's.

"Trump has sold me, what more can I say?" Lynn told a Reuters reporter before attending a Trump rally in Rock Hill, South Carolina.

Ms. Lynn, 83, is still as beautiful and talented as ever. She performs between eight to ten shows a month and doesn't miss an opportunity to Stump for Trump at the end of each show. She officially declared her support for him at an awards dinner in New York in early December.

She said "her audiences generally respond warmly to her cheers for Trump, and that's unusual. When you get up there and try to say you want to see Hillary Clinton win, that wouldn't go over so big,"

Other Republicans can't live up to Donald Trump, Lynn said, but stated Texas Senator Ted Cruz was her second choice.

Very pragmatically, Ms. Lynn clarified with "but when you're advertising for the best, forget the rest!"

Loretta Lynn wants to campaign for Donald Trump, however she has no plans to contact his campaign. "I just think he's the only one who's going to turn this country around," she said, but added "I'm going to let him call me.[88]"

Clint Eastwood is a true American patriot who loves to make pro-American films such as "American Sniper", the box office smash hit about NAVY Seal Chris Kyle. This wonderfully brilliant and moving movie about the hardships that our brave men and women endure when they are on the front line such as he was. I saw it with my husband and my Uncle Larry, a war vet and his wife. We were all touched by the struggles we witnessed. Eastwood brought all this to life on the big screen.

We are familiar with the "Empty Chair" routine Eastwood did when he addressed the 2012 Republican National Convention. The question-and-answer session with the chair — which was supposed to be about what Eastwood would ask President Obama in an interview — turned out to be hilarious. It was a moment we all loved as he mocked President Obama, making us all giggle, if not downright belly laugh.[89]

But now, Clint Eastwood is sharing his opinion on Donald Trump in a huge way. Not only does Eastwood support him, but he's speaking on behalf of Trump in California, Arizona, and Nevada.

In a recent interview, the American Sniper director was asked who he feels would serve America well and with a subtle emphasis on the campaign of Donald Trump, Eastwood stated this, "I think people are looking for somebody who is outspoken and who isn't afraid. And he seems to have kind of a fearless attitude."

However, Eastwood does give a nod to a few other too, saying he believes Ben Carson is a "common sense guy" and gives Ted Cruz and Marco Rubio high marks as well while still waiting to see who emerges victorious from the GOP-hopeful crowd of candidates.

He didn't pass up the opportunity to mock Barack Obama one more time by saying "Any one of them would be better than what we've got.[90]"

Willie Robertson, Businessman and star of A&E's "Duck Dynasty" gave his support to Trump at a September 25, 2015 rally in Oklahoma. He was invited to join the billionaire on stage at the Oklahoma State Fairgrounds in Oklahoma City.

"Willie! Get over here! Look at this guy! Look at this guy! Willie do you love Trump?" the 2016 Republican front-runner asked.

Robertson appeared sporting his signature long beard and camouflage, responded with, "I do like me some Trump, I gotta admit."

"Here's the deal", Robertson said, "We're both successful businessmen. We both have pretty big shows on television, we both have wives that are 1,000 times better looking than us so, I like Trump."

Robertson also appeared with Trump at the Outdoor Sportsman Awards in Las Vegas, where he introduced Trump to the crowd.

"The man I have the honor of introducing is not afraid to tell it like it is, he's not very politically correct, he's very bold, he loves his country and he firmly stands behind the Second Amendment,"

Robertson added, "I'm not talking about my father, OK? Phil's not here, he had to cruise on back to Louisiana, so he's unfortunately missing this event."

But no one expected Robertson's father, Phil Robertson, to be at that event, Phil Robertson has endorsed Ted Cruz.[91]

That must make for some very lively conversations in the Duck Dynasty household.

Mike Tyson, former heavyweight champion, officially gave Donald Trump his endorsement while appearing on HuffPost Live on Monday, 10/26/2015.

"He should be president of the United States," Tyson told HuffPost Live's Alex Miranda during a conversation about his Adult Swim show "Mike Tyson Mysteries."

Tyson said he's looking for a new, business-minded leader for the country after Obama's eight years in office.

"Let's try something new. Let's run America like a business, where no colors matter. Whoever can do the job, gets the job," Tyson said.

As for what Trump has said about immigration, Tyson said the words were "crude" but he said he doesn't believe Trump actually "thinks of Latinos in that way."

When Miranda asked Tyson if he officially endorses Trump, the former boxer gave a resounding response.

"I would [endorse him], yeah. I like Trump," he reiterated.[92]

Stephen Baldwin, a terrific actor, was fired by Trump on two different seasons of "The Celebrity Apprentice,". In spite of that, Baldwin told Don Lemon on a July episode of "CNN Tonight" that Trump would make a "great" president "because he's not a politician, and he doesn't care what anybody thinks."

Baldwin went on to explain, "He's saying what he thinks. And he's, you know, obviously, he said something the wrong way, recently, but what he said has now ripped the scab off of that issue. Everybody's talking about it. I golfed with about eight hedge fund guys today who said we really like what he's saying. Hedge fund guys."

Lemon then asked Baldwin if he thought Trump would win over everyday Americans? Then Baldwin stated, "I think every day Americans like him not just because of the celebrity. I think he's speaking his mind and that's refreshing.[93]"

Stephen Baldwin is right. It's Donald Trump's honesty and straight-forwardness that draws the masses to hear him speak. Americans know their politicians have been lying to them for years and to hear Trump tell the truth, good and bad, well, that's what we have been craving from our politicians but not getting.

Gary Busey, American actor, endorsed Trump back in 2011, even after being fired from season four of "The Celebrity Apprentice," and offered his praise for the presidential hopeful again this year. Right after his "Dancing with the Stars" debut, Gary Busey told FOX411 how much he believes in the Presidential candidacy of Donald Trump.

"He's a great guy. He's sharp. He's fast," he went on to say, "He can change the country after the last eight years."[94]

Photograph provided by Gage Skidmore

Anthony Mackie, In the liberal world of Hollywood, it's incredibly risky to come out as a Donald Trump supporter. This is even more true for black actors.

While promoting his new movie Our Brand Is Crisis, African American actor Anthony Mackie revealed that he is in fact a Trump supporter. It didn't take long for the liberal media to slam him for expressing this view.

"I would 100 percent want to run Trump's campaign. 100 percent." Mackie said, according to BET. "I mean, first that'll be the best party ever when he wins, and second, Trump's an easy sell. When you look at Trump, he's an easy sell because you can sell him as the guy who worked his way up from nothing. And I think if you're a 'pull yourself up by your bootstraps' candidate, people would identify with that."

"I'm on the bandwagon," he added. "I'm drinking the Kool-Aid!"

Hollywood has quickly turned on Mackie, with liberals slamming the actor for "turning on blacks" by supporting a candidate like Trump. We, however, support Mackie for expressing his conservative views in such a public way![95]

Dennis Rodman, retired pro-basketball player, tweeted on July 24, 2015, "@realDonaldTrump has been a great friend for many years. We don't need another politician, we need a businessman like Mr. Trump! Trump 2016."

Like so many before him, Rodham was fired during season two of "The Celebrity Apprentice, by Donald Trump."[96]

    Lou Ferrigno, an American actor, fitness trainer, and retired professional bodybuilder is best known for his title role in the CBS television series The Incredible Hulk.

    I first came to know Lou Ferrigno through the 1975 documentary Pumping Iron.[97] I must have watched it half a dozen times and Ferrigno became famous with the first airing.

    Ferrigno was asked by TMZ for his thoughts on Trump, and he said, "I hope Donald goes all the way." Ferrigno was also fired from a season of "The Celebrity Apprentice' by Donald Trump.[98]

Hulk Hogan, a professional wrestler, actor, and television personality was interviewed by TMZ in August of 2015. They asked Hogan which 2016 Republican presidential candidate he would want to face in the ring, but instead of answering the question, he simply says "He wants to Make America Great Again, by running with Donald Trump."

Hogan thinks the country may finally be ready for a Vice President Hogan.[99] Interesting thought.

Jesse James, star of the reality TV show Monster Garage and a onetime Celebrity Apprentice contestant, endorsed his old "boss" Donald Trump on his Facebook page, West Coast Choppers.

He writes at length about his experiences in living with Trump while filming the show.

He moved to NYC for 6 weeks and spent every day with Donald Trump, Ivanka Trump, and Don Jr. He explains "I really had no expectations. I think I was actually the only "Celebrity" that had a semi normal manual labor job. I think this gave me a very different perspective on things."

"I actually think Donald Trump had no idea who I was or what I actually did for a living but over the next month I was able to observe him and his kids in their day to day routine." James says of Trump "What I saw was a person that treated everyone with respect. Even the (Hispanic) guys in the mail room. He had coffee from the coffee machine and BS'd with them every single morning."

"Trash men and cops would stop him on the street and he would stop whatever he was doing and spend a little bit of time with every one of them. As the month went on I used my hard work and perseverance to gain the respect of the Trumps and most everyone around me."

James wrote. "This guy is the Real Deal, and will Make America Great Again."[100]

Ted Nugent, an American musician, singer, songwriter, hunter, and political activist, wrote an amazing article for WND in August of 2015, shortly after Mr. Trump announced his intended run. In it he explains quite eloquently why Americans are listening to Mr. Trump.

Nugent writes, "Donald Trump is running strong in the early polls because Americans are fed up with the political status quo, especially from left-leaning GOP Fedzillacrats who want to feed us cow dung while telling us it's a cheeseburger."

He goes on to explain, "Our forefathers wouldn't recognize the political labyrinth our professional politicians have created. The very things our forefathers warned us not to do as it pertains to embracing a centralized, powerful federal government is the very cliff our professional politicians have steered the Goodship America straight off of."

"Donald Trump's message sings to Americans because he doesn't play politically correct brain-dead games. He calls them like he sees them. That's refreshing to millions of Americans who believe political correctness is a public cancer that has eroded free speech and everything else good about America."

Lastly, Nugent's advice for Mr. Trump, "Carry on, Mr. Trump. Unless you are taking flak, you're not over the target.[101]"

I couldn't have said it any better Ted Nugent.

Jesse Ventura, the former pro wrestler, former Minnesota governor, and actor was speaking with Alex Jones when Ventura said, "Obama has been a big disappointment" but his biggest take-away from the Obama presidency is this "The fact that whether it is a Republican or whether it is a Democrat, it makes no difference. With these two parties, it does not make any difference which one gets elected, the same foreign policy will be carried out and probably, pretty much the same domestic policy will be carried out regardless."

The former pro wrestler was speaking with previous Trump staffer Roger Stone for "Off the Grid," when Ventura said, "I shocked my staff today. I came in and said, 'You know what, as far as the Republicans are concerned, I hope Trump wins'".[102]

Charlie Sheen, After initially tweeting this "Trump you're a sad & silly homunculus (sic) your words as poignant as a sack of cat farts You're a shame pile of idiocy",[103] Sheen eventually saw the light, boarded the Trump Train by tweeting out a month later that he'd be Trump's "VP in a heartbeat!"[104]

Ivana Trump, Socialite and Donald Trump's first wife recently held a luncheon in support of her ex-husband. There were about 40 friends in attendance for a two-hour luncheon that ended with the former Mrs. Trump endorsing his White House bid.

"She got up and thanked all of her friends for coming and then led a cheer. She said, 'Who's voting for Donald?' and we all raised our hands and said, 'Yay!' " said her longtime pal Nikki Haskell.

"They were all very pro-Donald. It was very high-spirited and very positive. Ivana did an amazing job," she said.[105]

Jeanine Pirro, former prosecutor, judge, and elected official from the state of New York, currently a legal analyst and television personality stated this in a surprise tweet, "I've been friends with Trump for years. Want to know why I support him? Find out this Podcast@ (Link: http://bit.ly/23EWprV)

Hershel Walker, retired NFL running back and former "Celebrity Apprentice" star has been a supporter of Trumps from the very beginning but in his latest interview with TMZ Sports, he reaffirms that support by saying "We have to quit being politically correct. I'm with Trump."

Herschel Walker saying he still believes Donald is the BEST MAN to be our next President.

With Trump coming under fire for his proposed plan to block Muslims from entering the U.S., TMZ Sports asked if he jumped ship.

The short answer was no, he's still with Team Trump all the way.

"Look, we can't build a wall and not let people in the country," Walker says "But we do have to get this country safe. We have to quit being politically correct."

"We have to do what's right to save America ... I guarantee you Donald would do better than a lot of people in office now. That I can tell you for a fact."

Trumps suggested temporary ban on Muslims has been controversial to say the least, but Walker states, "Donald has said what he's said, but his numbers haven't gone down. That's a sign he is saying the things that people think, but are afraid to say themselves. Donald is saying what people want to hear."[106]

At the end of the day, Walker says Trump still has his support.

University of Iowa football players include:
C.J. Beathard and Peter Pekar (unable to locate photo)

According to the NCAA's Advertising and Promotional Guidelines, student athletes are not allowed to appear in any advertisement that "endorses a political candidate or party, or ... advocates a viewpoint on controversial issues of public importance."

In spite of that, Donald Trump was endorsed today by several players from the University of Iowa Hawkeye football team at his rally in Iowa City, Iowa on January 26,2016.

On Tuesday, members of the Iowa football team endorsed Donald Trump at a rally at the University of Iowa.

The duo endorsing Trump, quarterback C.J. Beathard, a native of Franklin, Tennessee, and tight end Peter Pekar, who hails from Greendale, Wisconsin, stood on stage before Trump arrived, throwing Trump's "Make America Great Again" caps into the crowd. Pekar brandished a black and gold Iowa jersey with a No. 1 and Trump's name emblazoned on the back.[107] Go Hawkeye

Mike Ditka, the retired NFL coach said of Trump, "I think that he has the fire in his belly to make America great again and probably do it the right way, I do like Trump" in an interview with the Chicago Sun-Times.[108]

Terrell Owens, the retired NFL wide receiver told TMZ Sports in June, who appeared on "Celebrity Apprentice" with Trump earlier this year says "he gained a TON of respect for Trump during their time on the show," and thinks "D.T. could do great things for the country as the man in charge."

"This may be what the country needs and Trump ... he's a guy who won't put up with B.S. and has what it takes to change how government is run."

"With that being said, Trump ... YOU'RE HIRED"

Owens adds, "Plus, as the president, Trump would be able to say he knows me and he likes me ... LOL!"[109]

Tila Tequila, model and reality TV star, posted a video on YouTube, published on Oct 13, 2015, entitled *DONALD TRUMP FOR PRESIDENT 2016!!!!!! DO IT!!!!*

In this lengthy video, she expressing her support for Trump. Ms. Tequila says that she first laughed at Donald Trump like everyone else but realized she was judging him in the same manner that she'd been judged and that was wrong. So she began to research his policies and listen closely to him and realized that "Trump is the Man". She explains, point by point, why she has decided that Donald Trump should "definitely be our next President."

She finishes with "Donald Trump for President, Love you guys.[110]"

If you haven't watched her video, I recommend you do. The link is in the footnote.

Mark Cuban — The Dallas Mavericks owner and "Shark Tank" investor has said Trump is "the best thing to happen to politics in a long, long time." Cuban added in an interview that Trump "says what's on his mind. He gives honest answers rather than prepared answers."

Gene Simmons — While the Kiss bassist and former "Celebrity Apprentice" contestant has criticized Trump's views on immigration and his "incendiary language," he's also called him a "good family man" and a "straight shooter."

Omarosa Manigault-Stallworth — Although the former "Apprentice" contestant says she's a "die-hard registered Democrat," she's taken to the airwaves to defend Trump, calling him the Tiger Woods of politics: "When Tiger got involved with golf, people who had never been watching or involved or interested in golf, they got engaged. That's what's happening with this Trump candidacy."

Chingy, an early 2000's rapper known for unforgettable hits as "*Right Thurr*," and "*Holidae Inn*," took to Twitter to endorse Donald Trump for president with tweets like these:

"Politics vs. society. People should understand that politics is a business just like the job you work at. I vote for @realDonaldTrump "YEP" 3,"

Being more than just a fickle supporter, in 2004, Chingy paid homage to Trump with his song *"Fall'n"* with "Doin' it like Donald Trump, I'm sendin' this one."

Chingy's solidified his support for Trump just days after Sarah Palin announced her endorsement with this tweet.

"@realDonaldTrump knows how to conduct business. This country is a business and needs to be ran by a businessman. It's not personal people!"[111]

Sean (P. Diddy) Combs & Kayne West, both famous rappers, have joined the Trump Train. In an interview with The Washington Post, Diddy said, "Donald Trump is a friend of mine, and he works very hard."

Robert Davi, actor, singer, director and writer penned an article for Breitbart in November of 2015, where he lends his support for Donald Trump.

He begins with "I cannot sit back and listen to the media continually outright defame Donald Trump. I will not remain silent any longer."

"I am watching the pundits and media hosts continually bash Donald Trump and call him a liar over his claim that Muslims in New Jersey were cheering and celebrating over the Towers coming down." (a fact that was later proven to be correct).

Davi believes "We should thank God that Trump is in this race. The media and the establishment are terrified. They all have their instructions and they are in lockstep. You see, my dear fellow Americans, if Trump wins the gig is up. He will set back the destruction of America, and the globalists are in a panic. They paint Trump and his supporters as racist and uneducated. Well, guess what, I am neither and I know quite a few people who are for Trump. Some will not openly come out and say they support him because they're afraid of being falsely labeled by some here in Hollywood."

And that my friends, is a very true statement, as the people of Hollywood have been brutal to Trump Supporters.

Davi finishes by saying "If Ronald Reagan was the Gary Cooper of politics, Trump is the John Wayne. So, pilgrim, I'd rather have a President Trump who tells it like it is than a deceiver who feeds us sugarcoated poison at bedtime, only to have us wake up dead.[112]"

The latest endorsement has come from Kid Rock on February 1, 2016 in an interview with Rolling Stone Magazine. In it, Rock said this, "I'm digging Trump. I feel like a lot of people, whether you're a Democrat or a Republican, feel like if you get Hillary or Bernie, or you get Rubio or Cruz or whoever, there's going to be the same s—t."

The renowned musician also told the publication he feels that Mr. Trump will end up winning the Republican nomination.

"To me, I'm just like, 'We gotta try something else.' and I'm not an expert at political science or anything. I do try to follow things, obviously. I'm a pretty good, taxpaying citizen of this country," he said.

Kid Rock concluded by adding, "Let the business guy in there. It's not really working too well running it not like a business. I mean, what business f—king survives when they're f—king broke?[113]"

Pardon the language.

Additional endorsements of Donald J. Trump include:

Reverend Jerry Falwell, Jr.

Liberty University president Jerry Falwell Jr., the son of the late televangelist, endorsed Donald Trump on Tuesday, January 26, 2016, giving the Republican front-runner the blessing of one of the evangelical community's biggest names just days before the Iowa caucuses.

In a statement announcing his endorsement, Falwell called Trump "a successful executive and entrepreneur, a wonderful father and a man who I believe can lead our country to greatness again.[114]"

The Reverend Falwell endorsement solidified over the course of several months, with the two exchanging private phone calls, according to those familiar with the process. By the end of last year, Falwell was publicly encouraging Trump, while still holding off on an official endorsement. Today, he changed all that. There is no more uncertainly, Jerry Falwell, Jr. Is solidly behind Donald Trump.

"Trump reminds me so much of my father," Falwell stated in a December 2015 interview with Fox News including a penchant to "speak his mind.".

Phyllis Schlafly

Arch-conservative and avowed anti-feminist hasn't just pledged her allegiance to Donald Trump - she's called him America's "last hope."

In a December WND exclusive interview, Schlafly spoke of being disillusioned with the Republican-controlled Congress and frustrated that they passed the recent 1.1 trillion Omnibus Budget Bill.

"This is a betrayal of the grassroots and of the Republican Party," Schlafly said in reference to the 2014 Landslide election in which Republicans were given control of the House and the Senate.

"We thought we were electing a different crowd to stand up for America, and they didn't. We're extremely outraged by what Congress has done. Nancy Pelosi couldn't have engineered it any better. I think the people are going to react by electing Donald Trump."

"It sounds like Donald Trump is the only one who has any fight in him," Schlafly said. "He will fight for the issues that we really care about and are very hot at the present time, such as the immigration issue. I don't see anyone else who's eager to fight."[115]

Franklin Graham

A Christian evangelist and missionary. He is president and CEO of the Billy Graham Evangelistic Association and of Samaritan's Purse, an international Christian relief organization.

Graham had this to say about President Obama in regards to the Iran negotiations 'President Barack Obama is determined to negotiate with the terrorist thugs of the Iranian regime. This historic capitulation to a hostile nation has to raise serious questions about which side Barack Obama really is on. Iran is not to be trusted."

Therefore, Rev. Franklin Graham posted his support for Donald Trump's firm stance against the negotiations with Iran by saying "The sanctions against this brutal, Islamic nation are the least we can do to one of America's biggest enemies."

As Rev. Graham pointed out, Trump was the only one sounding the alarm on pastor Saeed Abedini, the American held prisoner in Iran since 2012. Rev. Graham says "His (Abedini's) wife and children haven't seen their husband and father in years, but Obama refuses to meet with them."[116]

For that reason, Graham took a leap of faith and announced his support of Trump on his Facebook page.[117]

Ann Coulter

An American conservative social and political commentator, writer, syndicated columnist, and lawyer was one of Trump's earliest supporters. She frequently appears on television, radio, and as a speaker at public and private events.

Coulter's latest book, *Adios, America: The Left's Plan to Turn Our Country Into a Third World Hellhole* was published on June 1, 2015. The book addresses illegal immigration, amnesty programs, and border security in the United States,[118] and was referenced by Donald Trump many times in his early rallies.

Ms. Coulter has been very outspoken in her support of Trump, telling WMAL in July, "Trump is different. We have been lied to for 30 years about immigration. That's why Trump is striking this chord. He's attractive. He's tall. He's hilariously funny. I think he could be not only a nominee who could win but a third party candidate who would win."[119]

Whether you agree with Ms. Coulter or not, one thing you can say is she's a woman with loads of passion, who will fight tooth and nail for the things she believes in. She is a force to be reckoned with and Donald Trump is lucky to have her on his side.

Michael Savage

"The Savage Nation" conservative radio host showed his support of the real estate billionaire's candidacy, stating in an interview that Donald Trump is the "Winston Churchill of our time,".

The Savage Nation" host opened his show with his admission that he was all-in for the real estate billionaire's candidacy before grilling him on the Iran nuclear deal, voter ID laws and his campaign goals.

Savage pledged his support by declaring "You're the lion… you're the Winston Churchill of our time. Keep hitting them real hard."[120]

Gavin McInnes, Vice Media's co-founder, better known these days for his controversial views on race and gender, has expressed support for Donald Trump.

In his hilarious but accurate video monologue published on You Tube, he says, the thing that sold him was Trump's proposed ban on Muslims entering the United States.

He passionately lays out his reasons for believing Trumps temporary ban on Muslims is necessary at this time in our history, by simply telling the truth of who these terrorist are and where they come from.

Intellectually, we already know everything he says in his videos to be true but because of political correctness, we aren't allowed to say them. Donald Trump gave us that voice back and Gavin McInnes thinks that's a good thing.

"I want to focus now on his most recent faux-pas, where he said we need to ban all Muslims from returning to America," McInnes said in the December video. "Pretty irrational, pretty brash, pretty crass. That's what we need in this day and age — we're at war."[121]

Sheriff Joe Arapaio, "America's Sheriff" is notorious for institutionalizing racial profiling in Maricopa County, Arizona.

The unlikely pair teamed up for a post-presidential debate victory rally drawing a crowd of thousands eager to hear the dynamic duo discuss illegal immigration together, on the same stage.

"You're the patriots, and you've got a lot of people, believe me, a lot of people won't say it, but they support Donald Trump. They won't tell you, but when they go into that voting booth, watch out," Sheriff Arapaio told a huge crowd as he introduced Mr. Trump at the rally. He says, "Trump is the clear choice for president, even if others won't admit it.[122]"

Today, January 26, 2016, Sheriff Joe Arapaio will appear with Trump at a rally in Marshalltown, Iowa, where he will give his official endorsement to Donald J. Trump.

In a statement from the Trump campaign released to The New York Times, Arapaio declared:

"Donald Trump is a leader. He produces results and is ready to get tough in order to protect American jobs and families. I have fought on the front lines to prevent illegal immigration and I know Donald Trump will stand with me, and countless Americans to secure our border. I am proud to support him as the best candidate for President of the United States of America.[123]"

Dana White

Businessman and entrepreneur. White is the current President of the Ultimate Fighting Championship (UFC), a mixed martial arts organization based in the United States but which operates globally. He is also a huge supporter of Donald Trump's.

The UFC mega-boss says he can't wait to get to the ballot box.

White, one of the most powerful people in sports, made no bones about it, he's Trump all the way, and he has his reasons.[124]

Diamond and Silk, These women are amazing. I've watched many of their videos posted to You Tube and they are truly Donald Trump's most fervent fans.

Azealia Banks, can always be counted on for saying and doing the unexpected.

The rapper took to Twitter in the early hours of Monday to say that she has made up her mind and plans to vote for Donald Trump.

AZEALIABANKS ✔@AZEALIABANKS

"Ok so, I think I'm ready to admit that I'm going to vote for Donald Trump."

2:17 AM - 1 Feb 2016

Zoltan Bathory, guitarist of Five Finger Death
Punch speaks about about his support for Trump and
gun rights.

He's a staunch supporter of gun rights, and spoke
about the issue in a 2014 interview. "The second
amendment makes all the other ones possible,"
Bathory explains. "But let's extend this; it's not just
about the rights that are given to you by a piece of
paper. When your life is in actual danger, you don't
care about any paper; you will just defend your life no
matter what it takes. It's about defending yourself and
your family. You should be able to do that."

Bathory continues, "Some people say that owning a
gun is uncivilized and brute, but we can look at that
issue from a completely different perspective; maybe
gun ownership actually made us more civilized, since
guns act as equalizers. All of a sudden a physically
superior person cannot simply abuse a weaker one,
since the gun will act as a deterrent."

Interestingly enough, Five Finger Death Punch
recently launched a contest to have fans remake their
"Jekyll and Hyde" single. One of the submissions

requirements is that the mixes must contain bits of Donald Trump's speeches within the song. Interesting idea and if you'd like to check out the remix, dubbed "Donald Death Punch (Jekyll and Hyde Trump Mix), posted by Pure Grain Audio at http://loudwire.com/five-finger-death-punch-zoltan-bathory-support-donald-trump/. Check it out.

Juanita Broaddrick, former nursing home administrator who publicly accused Bill Clinton of rape in 1999 has come out in support of Donald Trump.

Broaddrick said that while she doesn't consider herself a member of either major political party, Republican presidential candidate Trump "says the things I like to hear," according to an interview with *The Hill*.[125]

Paula Jones, former Arkansas state employee who also accused Bill Clinton of rape says she is furious that Clinton is campaigning for his wife Hillary Clinton is her bid for the White House.

In an interview with *The Hill*, Ms. Jones states that she, "counts herself among the fans of Republican presidential candidate Donald Trump."

"I like Donald Trump!" the former tabloid fixture, who sued then-President Bill Clinton in 1994 for sexual harassment, says in excerpts provided by "Inside Edition" from an interview airing Thursday.

"I'm going to vote for the person who I think is best for our country, and to get it back on track, and the person who can be trusted," Jones adds. "Somebody who is from the heart and is a truthful person and loves our country.[126]"

Adam Curry, political commentator and former MTV VJ unequivocally stated his support during "Audio: No Agenda Episode 741 - Bad Optics" by stating this, "I, Adam Curry, am as of today, officially, officially announcing my full support my endorsement, my coveted endorsement ... for Donald Trump for Republican candidate for the Presidency of the United States of America".[127]

Ted DiBiase, former professional wrestler stated this about Donald Trump in a blog post, "The character would probably vote for Donald Trump because he's a billionaire and the real Ted DiBiase would also vote Trump because he's not swayed by money. You don't become a billionaire by being an idiot. If he doesn't know, he's smart enough to surround himself with the right people who do know.[128]"

Jim Gilchrist, leader and co-founder of the Minuteman Project had these words to say in an article he wrote on August 3, 2015.

"Dear Americans,
I have long held that the illegal alien population in the United States hovers just above 30 million…about 10% of the nation's population.
The annual cost to subsidize such a huge impoverished population is about $380 BILLION annually. That's almost 1/2 TRILLION dollars annually!
Go figure why the USA is $18 TRILLION in debt after so many decades of encouraging the transfer of poor and unskilled masses from Mexico and Central America (and other countries, too) into the United States.

US taxpayers are required to pay off this enormous debt with increased tax levies in the future. Not just income tax increases, but increases in sales taxes, real estate taxes, DMV fees, excise taxes on utilities and telephones, and various other increased surtaxes, etc., etc...with no end in sight.

Donald Trump appears determined to bring our nation back under the rule of law insofar as U.S. immigration laws are concerned.

Americans, please join me in endorsing Donald Trump for president 2016. Furthermore, I think Texas Senator Ted Cruz is an excellent pick for vice president. These two candidates think the same, talk the same...and, hopefully will walk the same once in the White House.

This is our last chance to elect a presidential administration that will finally take on the enormous task of returning America to its heralded status as a "nation of laws.[129]"

Alex Jones, radio talk show host defends Donald Trump on December 8, 2015. states that "Donald Trump is right, we need to have a total and complete shutdown of everyone coming from a long list of nations who have not been properly vetted. But the federal government will allow people in with fake passports, name and addresses like the Saudi Arabian Jihad Princess who was clearly involved in the San Bernardino attacks last week."

Mr. Jones says that our country has reached crazy proportions without any regard to National Security. You can watch his tantalizing video on You Tube.[130] Mr. Jones gets it.

Wayne Allyn Root, businessman, politician, television and radio personality wrote this about Trump, "Love him or hate him, only Donald Trump has the chutzpah, audacity, street smarts, killer instincts and vicious lawyers to fight Hillary Clinton and win. This isn't about who won a debate because he or she had a better grasp of details. No CEO is a details guy. Donald isn't a details guy. Details are left to policy wonks and think tanks. This is a battle to save America."

"Trump has the audacity and willingness to investigate and prosecute Democrats who have run roughshod over the U.S. Constitution. I'm not as worried about Trump's conservative principles as I am excited by the prospect of making Obama, Hillary, Eric Holder, Valerie Jarrett, Jonathan Gruber (the architect of the Obamacare fraud), and top IRS officials pay for their crimes against the American people and violations of the Constitution."

"This is the exact pledge Trump should run on. The American people, including the millions of conservative and working class voters who stayed home for John McCain and Mitt Romney, will come out in record numbers to support anyone promising to put the criminals in the Obama administration in prison.[131]"

Milo Yiannopoulos, journalist and political commentator appeared on Sky News today to debate whether Donald Trump would be a good choice for US President, telling presenter Kay Burley that Trump would make America "fabulous again."

Yiannopoulos debated Kate Andrews from the ASI, who was more skeptical about whether Trump is presidential material.

Andrews and Burley suggested that Trump had a problem with "hurtful" statements about women and minorities but Yiannopoulos pointed out that Trump is polling strongly with blacks, Hispanics and women.

"Is he a misogynistic racist?" asked Burley.

"Of course not," responded Yiannopoulos, who went on to say: "You can't stump the Trump. He'll make America fabulous again.[132]"

February 17, 2016, Donald Trump was endorsed by the Low Country Sportsmen at a huge rally in Walterboro, South Carolina in front of thousands of cheering fans.[133]

AN AMERICAN LOVE-FEST

MORE EXCITING THAN A ROCK CONCERT

On October 10th of 2015, I attended my first-ever campaign rally in Duluth, Ga with my husband, Greg, and my uncle, retired Veteran Larry Atchley. I had no idea what to expect as we approached the venue in my uncles new truck which proudly displays a Purple Heart license plate, but that belies the fact that he's one of the most humble people I've ever known.

We arrived three hours early and were somewhat disappointed to see that we were not the first ones there. Others had beat us, making us about 60th in line. The day was so hot and there was virtually no shade to speak of, so we all sat there trying to entertain ourselves, as we baked like potatoes in the oven. But that was nothing compared to later.

While we waited in line, Greg bought me a light blue "Make America Great Again" hat from a vendor nearby. It was hot so I pulled my long hair up in a rubber-band and put on my new hat. It gave me a small bit of relief and at this point, anything was a help. We bought Trump buttons and bumper stickers from a different vendor who was walking up and down the ever-growing line of Trump Supporters.

It wasn't long before I couldn't see the end of the line any longer but I was told that it wrapped out of the parking lot and around the block.

As the time approached for the doors to be opened, my uncle took the folding chairs he'd brought to the truck only a few feet away. He jumped back in line with us just in time to head for the door.

We sailed through the door, without having to forfeit our printed tickets, easily gaining entrance to the building.

My husband was distressed to see an apparent lack of security measures being taken and he instantly became concerned for Mr. Trumps safety. There are some really desperate people out there who would love to stop our front-runner anyway they can.

As I mentioned earlier, my husband has cancer and since he really wanted to go, I called the venue ahead of time to see if seating was available. There was and Greg headed straight for the seats, while Larry and I lost track of each other in our desperate flight to the front of the stage. As it turned out, he and I both got right in front, just on opposite sides of the podium. Donald Trump would stand directly between us both, a mere few feet away. How fortunate was that?

Even though they let us in, there was still two hours until Mr. Trump was to appear. In that time, I got to know the people around me very well.

I was pleased to meet three young men, all age 19, and they were just as excited as I was to be there. I met a couple with their 8 year old girl waving her Trump banner proudly, while sitting on her father's shoulders.

As I looked around the convention hall mainly trying to spot Greg, I was amazed at the diversity with which this group represented.

I saw the young, the elderly and every age in between; men, women and families. I spoke with a disabled woman in a wheelchair and her care-giver, who defied the odds, just to see our next President. Amazingly enough, she made it to the front of the venue, right next to me.

I saw many Veterans, like my Uncle, so proud of their country and eager to see our next Commander in Chief.

I saw Asians, Hispanics, Black and White Americans and even some Middle Easterners. It felt like all of America was represented at that rally, even Gay America, as one of the young men I spoke to volunteered that information.

We were all there, clustered like sardines, willing to endure the most miserable conditions, just to see Donald Trump.

As the original two hour wait inside the venue dragged into the third, the room was becoming really uncomfortable. I've always been mildly claustrophobic and the anxiety I felt here was only kept at bay by my excitement to see Donald Trump. The tightness was difficult at best, but the growing heat of the room was becoming intolerable. October in Georgia is typically stifling but this day was exceptionally so.

There was air conditioning in the venue but with all those bodies, it seemed as if there wasn't. Thank goodness they didn't take our tickets at the door because that was the only thing I had to fan my sweating face with now.

I could feel the sweat trickle down my back and I believe this room is hotter than any room I'd ever been in before.

I could hear those around me complaining that their backs were hurting; at least I had the bike rail in front of me to lean on, others had nothing.

Thousands of strangers packed together in less than favorable conditions would typically bring out the worst in people, but not at a Trump Rally.

The excitement of the people in that room was palpable, it was electric and it was energizing. It kept this claustrophobic woman of 52 from fleeing, even though my instinct was to do just that.

As soon as I saw Trump's security detail, I knew it was about to begin. The man we'd come to see, the one I'd waited six hours for, was finally going to arrive.

The energy in the room began to grow as others noticed it too and when the curtain finally parted and Donald Trump walked into the room, the crowd went wild.

I've been to dozens of rock concerts in my life, from Madonna to David Bowie, but the energy in this room exceeded even those.

When Trump took the stage, you felt his presence as much as saw it. He's a magnetic force, that draws you in and when he spoke, it was like he was speaking directly to me.

There were thousands of people in the small convention center, but I do believe that Trump made eye contact with each one of us, at least all that he could.

Donald Trump has been speaking for nearly an hour and he's sweating almost as much as the rest of us. I was close enough to see the glistening beads trickle down his face, as he remarked at the heat of the south.

My back was breaking and my silky blouse stuck to me like glue from the moisture in the room, but I didn't want it to end. I could've stood there listening to Mr. Trump speak all day.

But the rally did end in typical Trump fashion, with his declaration that together, we would "Make America Great Again."

The music began to play, the crowd began to cheer all the while waving Trump banners high above their heads.

I videoed Mr. Trump descending the stairs from the stage, but instead of turning to go behind the curtain, he headed in our direction. He stopped at the first of his fans, shaking hands and signing autographs. He was going to walk down the line and that meant right in front of me.

The next thought that popped into my head was an autograph, did I dare hope to get one? I watched as Mr. Trump slowly walked the line, getting closer, as I frantically began to search for something for him to autograph. I hadn't brought anything inside with me and all I had was this banner, which I'd torn just a bit, but I guess it would have to do.

I put my cell phone in the pocket of my jeans when Donald Trump was two people from me. He was standing in front of a young woman who obviously had the same problem I did. What to get him to sign? Then she decided. She ripped her shirt-sleeve back, exposing her upper arm. Everyone watched as Mr. Trump signed his name on her bare skin.

I had to laugh but it was an idea. Then another thought came to mind. If he signed there, I'd never be able to bathe again and I didn't think my family would be okay with that.

So instead, it was the banner and I got it ready as Trump signed a book for the gentleman next to me.

I felt a trickle begin at my brow and instinctively I raised my tired arm to wipe the sweat away. I felt something hard and the dawning realization of what it was delighted me. It was the brim of my brand new, baby blue, "Make America Great Again" hat. Just as Mr. Trump left the man next to me I snatched it from my head and met Donald Trump, eye to eye.

He smiled at me and I smiled back as I greeted our next President with a humble "Hello Mr. Trump." He thanked me for coming as I handed my hat to him.

He remarked about having not seen the baby blue hats yet and I told him it was one of my favorite colors. He took hold of the brim of my hat as his security man whispered something in his ear. He tilted his head in that direction and listened but he never took his eyes off me. For a few seconds Donald Trump and I both had hold of that hat and it was like something electric passed through me.

All the aching, all the sweating, the claustrophobia, the now eight hours of standing with no bathroom break, the misery I went through to get to that moment, was all forgotten, washed away by the energy that I now drew from Donald Trump.

He signed my hat, thanked me again and shook my hand before he moved on to the now forgotten person beside me.

I stood for a moment stunned as the crowd began to disperse from around me. I couldn't believe it. Elated, I stared at the autographed hat in my trembling hands, then went in search of my husband and my uncle.

I felt fortunate to have been at that particular rally because it was large enough to be exciting while intimate enough to feel like I was one-on-one with the man of the hour.

Larry and I also went to the Trump Rally on Nov 30, 2015 in Macon, Georgia. We drove two hours and arrived six hours before the doors even opened. We were the first car in line and the first ones to arrive at the doors. As soon as we got there, I tweeted out "First in line at Trump Rally In Macon, Ga. six hours early. Whoo hoo!" So silly, I know. For about an hour, Larry and I were the only two there besides all the Trump staff.

We met Jeanne Seaver, a Trump Georgia employee, who was in charge of the event coordination that day. She's a lovely woman, tall and blond and she was kind enough to allow Larry and me to park ourselves at her table, securing our first place in line.

Soon others began to arrive. I met a very nice woman, Barbara, who was about my age and a father with his teen-aged son. A charming young man who was thrilled to be attending a Donald Trump Rally. He brought with him a copy of "The Art Of The Deal" hoping to get Mr. Trump to autograph it.

The crowd began to grow and before long, the vendors and the media arrived. Barbara and I walked over to a t-shirt vendor to buy pink Donald Trump shirts. I had mine hanging over my arm while she was waiting for them to dig out her size medium.

We were chattering, not paying attention to who was around us when I said to Barb "I haven't been this excited since I was a young girl at a rock concert." We laughed and she agreed as she reached for her t-shirt. We walked back to Larry and sat down at the table, settling in for what was still a very long wait.

Just then, I felt a tap on my shoulder. I looked to my left, where a very short woman with shoulder length brown hair was standing next to a large man who held an even larger camera.

This female reporter from Fox5 News said to me, "I just over-heard you say you haven't been this excited since you were a young girl at a rock concert." To which I replied "That's right." She wanted to know why.

Before I knew what was happening, the camera was rolling and I was talking. I said a lot of things and after it was over, I thought that with all these people here there was little chance that this southern girl would make it on the air, so I forgot about the incident and went back to enjoying my second rally experience.

They opened the doors and Larry and I ran inside, only to be funneled through metal detectors. This time security was tight, with Secret Service surveying the crowd and police officers with hand-held scanners and bomb sniffing dogs.

Since we arrived so early, we'd overheard the staff talking about the tight security, so I'd emptied my pockets of everything except some chap stick and bubble-gum.

I sailed through the metal detectors and was the first person on the floor of the arena. I secured a place for Larry and me right in front of the podium.

I slung my pink Trump t-shirt over the bike rail and waited for Larry who had gotten stuck at the metal detectors. He told me later that they made him turn on his cell phone, just to make sure it was real.

The rally was the typical Love-fest that I've seen play out across the nation, but this one was particularly exciting for my Uncle Larry, because Donald Trump singled him out, the retired-veteran, from the stage.

Trump was talking about "Taking the Oil" and giving the money to the wounded warriors, when he points straight at my Uncle, who is next to me in the front row, and says, "In the old days, 'To the victor', you know, you're a military man, I can see it. Stands up straight, great guy. But I can see it. To the victor belongs the spoils. Right?".

Larry nods to Mr. Trump and says "Yes Sir, I do." as he indeed stood there shoulders back, head held high, as I beamed standing there next to him.

At the end of the Rally, Larry and I waited patiently for our turn to see Donald Trump. Larry didn't get an autograph at the Norcross rally like I did, so we wanted to make sure he got one this time.

When it came our turn, Larry stood proudly face to face with Donald Trump. As Mr. Trump signed Larry's hat, he thanked him, my Uncle, for his service to our country. It is one of my Uncle's proudest moments.

I got two more autographs myself, the banner and my pink T-shirt so now I can't wear the T-shirt. Oh well. My collection now looks like this:

Larry and I left the venue, so excited to have met Donald Trump once again.

I got home and ran into the house to tell Greg about the day but before I could say a word, my adoring husband announces that he saw his beautiful wife on TV. I stopped in my tracks as the horror swept over me.

We didn't have cable TV in our house so for Greg to have seen it, he had to have watched it on the Internet. I asked him "How could you possibly know about that?" I hadn't told him, then with a sweet little smirk, he told me that one of my girlfriends, Tracy, saw it on TV and told everyone on Facebook about it.

Well, that shock was bad enough but when I watched the clip, I was horrified. That woman from Fox 5 News took little snippets of what I said and made me look like the biggest southern hick there ever was.

The next time I see a giant camera coming at me with a squatty little dark haired woman beside it, I am running the other way, as fast as I can. That had to be the worst moment of my life.

Mark Allen is still reeling from the excitement of a Trump Rally. These are his words:

"HI, I JUST GOT BACK FROM A DONALD TRUMP RALLY AND LET ME TELL YOU SOMETHING, I AM STILL ENERGIZED..THAT MAN IS AMAZING IN PERSON...YOU HAVE GOT TO ATTEND ONE TRUMP RALLY...HE IS THE NICEST MAN I HAVE EVER MET... OH MAN...I WAS 10 FEET FROM HIM. I WAITED 5 HOURS AND BOY WAS IT WORTH IT....I SHOOK HIS HAND AND HE AUTOGRAPHED THIS PEACE FLAG I PAINTED TWO DAYS AGO TO TAKE...OH MAN, I'M STILL ENERGIZED...I CANT IMAGINE HIM NOT BEING THE NEXT PRESIDENT...HE'S LIKE FAMILY ONCE YOU MEET HIM. YOU JUST DON'T WANNA LEAVE...I WILL BE TALKING ABOUT MY EXPERIENCE FOR THE NEXT YEAR TO PEOPLE. AND, I HAVE HIS AUTOGRAPH TO PROVE I WAS THERE ...OH MAN, PLEASE GO TO A RALLY OF DONALD TRUMPS BEFORE YOU DECIDE WHO TO VOTE FOR...YOU WILL NOT BE THE SAME PERSON. I GUARANTEE IT...I PROMISE YOU...I LOVE THAT MAN AND O GOSH, DONALD TRUMP AS PRESIDENT WOULD ROCK THIS WORLD FOR THE BETTER. YOU WILL BE PROUD ...TRUST ME..."

Mark Allen's personal photo posted to Facebook on February 16, 2016.[134]

Avatar: diskus girl:

"I attended a Trump rally with 2 of my sons and their friends. the place was packed 14,000 and half the audience was under 30!!!

The progressive America haters have ruined their Country and they know they are going nowhere in a centrally planned Amerika. God Bless Donald!"

THE COUNTRY RALLIES WITH DONALD TRUMP

Rally in Phoenix, Arizona on July 11, 2015, less than one month after his announcement.

YUGE Rally in Mobile, Alabama on August 21, 2015 where an estimated 30,000 attended.

Dallas Rally held on September 14, 2015

The Rally in Norcross, Georgia, thousand packed into the small Convention Center. I was there.

Donald Trump gives a speech aboard the World War II Battleship USS Iowa, September 15, 2015, in San Pedro, California.

Amazing Rally!
Jacksonville, FL on October, 24, 2015

Donald Trump speaks in Springfield, Illinois
Nov. 9, 2015 to a crowd of more than 10,000

I was at this Rally in Macon, GA on Nov 30, 2015,
where my Uncle took this photograph.

Donald Trump Rally In Michigan on December 21, 2015 where Trump begins calling out the cameramen to "pan the crowd".

January 2, 2016 Rally in Biloxi, Mississippi

Trump greets the crowd after the Biloxi Rally.

Donald Trump speaks to supporters during a
campaign event at Clemson University in Pendleton,
S.C. on February 10, 2016.

WHO ARE TRUMP SUPPORTERS?

Who are the people showing up in droves, waiting for hours to hear what Donald Trump has to say? He has some of the most loyal supporters ever seen in politics, so I wanted to know, who are these people and why do they support this man so completely.

The media calls them racist, ignorant, low-information voters. They are mocked, demeaned and the vulgarity they endure from celebrities and comedians, is insulting to say the least.

When you are "outed" as a Trump supporter, you are immediately labeled a nut-case, deranged, devoid of all humanity but that couldn't be further from the truth.

I found that supporters of Donald Trump are just everyday men and women, young and old, all frustrated with the country's current direction. Regardless of race, religion or nationality, if they are citizens of this country, they are fearful that the America they love is disappearing before their eyes. They worry for the security of their children and they want America taken back from the devastation of Political Correctness and they want to give the next generation a better America than they were handed.

Trump is thriving by superbly tapping into the fears and anxieties that have emerged in an extremely distrustful society.

The people pledging allegiance to Mr. Trump come from all corners of the nation. They work in restaurants, offices, retail stores and run small businesses. They come from both political parties and some have never bothered to vote in the past, but they plan to this time.

They are young 17 and 18 year olds who are voting for the first time and they are our elderly and our retired who never miss an election. They are wounded warriors, veterans and our protector's in blue. They are professionals and blue collar workers. They are you and me, they could be anyone.

They love that Trump speaks his mind and they don't care if he uses profanity while speaking to the masses at a rally. They love his attitude, one supporter said he "loved that Donald Trump just doesn't seem to give a f---."

Trump's bombastic rhetoric and hard-line stance on immigration is exactly what the people of this country want to hear. They see illegal immigrants "breaking the law" and it infuriates them because they know, sometimes first-hand, that as a legal citizen of this country, they wouldn't get away with breaking the law like illegals do every day.

They'd go straight to jail, do not pass go, whereas illegal immigrants caught perpetrating sometimes horrific crimes, like killing beautiful Kate Steinle or so many others, are given a free pass, health-care and an EBT card. American's are sick of having to play by the rules while the rest of the world takes advantage of our generous if not naive attitudes toward humanity as a whole.

Not only are illegal immigrants flooding our porous Southern border, coming in with them are untold numbers of Radical Islamic Terrorist. After the San Bernardino terrorist attacks, perpetrated by two radicalized individuals, there was only one candidate

who made the promise to America to "bomb the sh--
out of ISIS".

This candidate exudes self-confidence and
leadership, a combination rarely found in today's
politicians. And he's not afraid to tell us, the American
people exactly what's really going on, whether we
want to hear it or not.

One beloved quality that Trump displays is his
apparent imperviousness to the boundaries that restrain
the permanent political class in our country. His
oftentimes provocative or inflammatory statements
on various topics like immigration, banning Muslims
and terrorism have angered some but accomplished
one thing. It forced these otherwise taboo topics into
the light and into the discussion.

Witnessing Donald Trump's bravery by speaking
the words that we've all been thinking but unable to
say, has shown us that what we've been fearing, the
things that have kept us quiet, were thrust upon us by a
small minority in this country, the Liberal Left and
corrupt politicians. Through fear and intimidation they
have kept us, the majority, silent but Donald Trump
has shown us that we don't have to be silent anymore.

And silent is one thing we will never be again,
Thank you Donald Trump.

These are discussions that Americans have wanted to have for some time but political correctness and "do nothing" politicians have kept these things off the table. Donald Trump ripped the band-aid off the wound and has put these painful truths out in front for everyone to see.

The following stories are from people who responded to my on-line survey. They come from all walks of life and live throughout the nation. I wanted to see through their eyes; to understand the remarkable rise of Donald Trump and just exactly what this love-fest between Trump and his loyal supporters was really all about.

Thousands upon thousands of people flock to Trump rallies everyday and they can't seem to get enough of him. They wait for six hours, sometimes longer, just to get into the building, while many thousands behind them are turned away by local Fire Marshals.

The stories you will hear were chosen from many but are reflective of the whole. They are brave people who wanted their words to be heard and I thank them all for their participation in my project.

What emerged from my exhaustive research was a clear picture of a powerful political movement. One quite possibly larger than the "Hope and Change" movement of Barack Obama in 2008.

This American Love-Fest with a politician is virtually unprecedented in modern day politics but it's real none-the-less.

Trump supporters are passionate and forgiving people and will come to Trump's defense, no matter the transgression.

Donald Trump knows how loyal his supporters are and has jokingly said this: "I could stand in the middle of 5th Avenue and shoot somebody and I wouldn't lose voters."

I grimaced when he said that but I also chuckled because Mr. Trump was on to something. Nobody cares what he says or how he says it, as long as he continues to tell them the truth. The American people have been lied to for decades and betrayed by the very politicians they put in power so the truth that comes from Donald Trump is intoxicating and the people are soaking it up.

The lying politicians said all the right words, they promised us that if we gave them power, they would stop the destructive agenda of the Obama Administration. They said they would repeal Obamacare, they said lots of things and we overwhelmingly believed them. We handed the Republicans a landslide victory in the 2014 Midterm Elections and they stabbed us in the back once again.

Is it any surprise that Donald Trump has garnered such wide-spread support? The people have had enough. They want Donald Trump for President because they believe, if elected, he will "Make America Great Again."

Avatar: cddBoze speaks to Trump supporters being called racist by the media. He says:

"You gotta love all Trump supporters being lumped together as racist a-holes. I support Trump and I am not racist or an a-holes. I want our country protected and to be given a chance to get itself out of the debacle known as Obama and rally. Nationalist = racist. So nice for all of us to be judged because we support a candidate who loves his country."

"One thing I hope Trump starts to bring up is for all those who came to the US in the early half of the 1900's (Italians, Greeks, Irish, Armenians, Portuguese, etc.) is that they came and they assimilated and embraced the United States and the American Dream. When libs say we are a country of immigrants- sure but those cultures came and were grateful for what the US offered and adapted to the cultural differences and did things like...stop the presses...learn English! They also worked their asses off to be successful. That's why the US has risen to being the number one world power. Hard work was encouraged and it meant a better life. Today's immigrant (not all but many) come illegally, never learn English, and sign up for government benefits. This needs to change. You want to come to the US? Assimilate, assimilate, assimilate. Otherwise, go back to where you came from and see how well your country treats you."

"I have relatives who fled the Genocide in Armenia and gave up all their massive wealth just for a chance to come to the US and prosper and they did. That mindset has been lost."

@USATrustTrump

Date: **1-10-16**
Age: **62, Hispanic Female who requested only that her Twitter handle be used.**
Lives in **McAllen, Texas**
Level of Education: **Masters(M.ED.)/B.A.-Social Work**
Party Affiliation: **Republican**
Political Leanings: **I describe myself as close to a neo-conservative ideology but with a limited interventionist foreign policy preference.**

She stayed at home and **didn't vote in 2012** due to poor options in both parties.

1. What is the first word that comes to mind when you hear the name Donald J. Trump?
Trustworthy

2. What do you consider Trump's strongest personal trait?
Mr. Trump is a strong leader and passionate man in everything he endeavors. His strength makes me feel safe, protected by my government who under a Trump presidency will have our interests in mind, and I feel a certain amount of certainty in my future as an American. He is decisive in the business world and on social and

political issues after he has studied issues or problem at hand. By the same token, he will not hesitate to regroup and change his mind on matters if facts deemed a need to change course while not caring what others think of his switch of opinion. His attitude is admirable. Most politicians will decide on issues and will not reevaluate positions even if ever-changing events or circumstances dictate that a change is deemed necessary so as to not appear inconsistent to the voters. Furthermore, if politicians change their mind on issues it is due to expectations of personal gain of some kind or to please their donors. Mr. Trump does the right thing and does not care what anyone thinks or what consequences his change of position will have on his ambitions to be President.

3. What do you consider Trump's weakest personal trait?

He can be sensitive at times and be somewhat hurt by attacks on him, his character, or about his political acumen. But, that is only because he is not a career politician and he has lead all his life as a skilled and gifted businessman so much that he has not become accustomed to the level of scrutiny like politicians receive on the campaign trail. Long standing and seasoned politicians have been trained or mentored to allow attacks to slide off their back and to focus on their goal which is to gain political power and influence for personal gain such as writing books every so many years. Book writing by politicians is the fastest way to make money and appear legitimate in doing so. You accept Mr.

Trump "as is" or you don't. I accept him 'as is' since he is one of us with his thorns and all but with a hidden genius undetected by many due to his simple nature about him.

4. How do you feel about Mr. Trump's family values. **Mr. Trump has strong and admirable family values. Merely listening to his adult children express how he taught them about work ethic and family unity says it all. One of Mr. Trump's family values appears to be the virtue of honest communication in all interactions. Mr. Trump daily models open and honest communication with family and all others which is one of the biggest qualities, I believe, that has won him support on the campaign trail from voters who distrust elected officials for good reason. He is consistent being forthcoming with everyone at all times unlike Mr. Cruz, another presidential candidate, who says one thing to supporters in one venue but behind closed doors will deviate from his original position to please his donors or voter positions. His children have also seem to have been taught courage to speak up and self-disciplined to aspire to be their highest self. Mr. Trump's family value teamwork and supporting each other. In one magazine interview it was revealed that Ivanka, daughter from one marriage, helped her half-sister, from another marriage, secure employment.**

5. Are you concerned with his past marriages and bankruptcies?

No, I am not concerned about Mr. Trump's past marriages and bankruptcies. The divorce rate in America is high and it would not be usual for a man his age to have had one or two marriages or even three. Mr. Trump has revealed in interviews with media that he believes in marriage and not just living together prompting him to marry making his relationships legitimate. Additionally, he acts responsibly as a parent caring for, and providing emotional and financial support to his children from the different marriages. Who cares about bankruptcies when one has become a billionaire many times over. Moreover, bankruptcies are legal ways to clear bad debt and a wise choice at times in the business sector.

6. Does it concern you that Mr. Trump was a Democrat before he was a Republican and has donated to both sides?

No, it does not bother me that Mr. Trump was a Democrat before he was a Republican and that he has donated to both political parties. I was a lifelong Democrat until 2008 when President Obama launched his presidential campaign. I knew then that supporting someone like Mr. Obama was not consistent with my political views and my values; thus, I voted Republican for the first time in 2008. In the future, I will vote for the candidate as a person and not along political lines since at times the trust for a certain candidate might not be there in a given political party. To clarify, I do lean Republican and agree much more with a conservative platform.

7. What concerns you most about the path our country is currently on?

Our country is in decline in all areas due to a lack of leadership for years now. We are at a crossroads and if we do not elect the right person for the Presidency we will become a country that is unrecognizable. Growing up for me was all about aspiring for the American Dream. Many of my peers succeeded due to their own efforts without government assistance of any kind. If you wanted a middle class lifestyle, it was within your reach if you received an education or training, were persistent, and ambitious. Without Trump taking us back to those times, there will be a government of free stuff to hand out and dependence on government. Even some middle class Americans today want a free college education for themselves or their children without even asking where the money to pay for such is coming from which I find appalling.

8. What do you expect to see from a Trump Presidency?

I expect a return to exceptionalism and greatness in America. The United States would be respected worldwide and our President Trump would be touted as a world class leader. We will return to being a great power in the world but not the policeman in the world.

He would not involve us in all world conflicts but instead pick and choose which international conflicts pose a threat to our freedom and way of

life. One of his favorite words to describe himself is "I'm smart." And, he is and I would trust him with my life and future.

He would focus on entrepreneurship as he seems to believe, as I do, that one can make it on our own efforts. In other words, I like many of his followers, believe in equal opportunity but not guaranteed equality of results.

I see him focusing on Americans learning self-discipline and self-responsibility versus a dependence of government programs which he will keep for those in emergency situations but government assistance would be temporary. He would ensure that our veterans, the elderly, and disabled receive more permanent help as needed.

I expect to see Mr. Trump engage in cleanup work in the White House, with federal agencies, and how Congress works with the U.S. President. I foresee him investigating some departments such as the IRS, Veterans Administration, and even the Department of Justice for ethics violations and/or criminal charges.

Mr. Trump would unite the American people and even the doubters would come around to respect him due to his comprehensive goals for America, his quick accomplishments that would be forthcoming, and how he has a culturally diverse team in his administration. I expect he will lead by example.

9. How would a President Trump help your family?
Our family would feel relief that we have a competent leader and it would encourage them to

set higher standards and personal goals for themselves as Mr. Trump has done his entire life. He is the perfect role model as a father, husband, businessman, and national leader and one my family would want to emulate and look up to for guidance.

10. Do you think Mr. Trump is straightforward with his plans for the country?

Unquestionably, I believe Mr. Trump is straightforward with his plans for the country. He is a straight shooter and has given thought for a long time, it seems, on what policies and practices would make America great again. Each time Mr. Trump speaks the listener knows he is speaking from his heart and is not at all rehearsed like the other presidential candidates.

11. In your opinion, would a President Trump secure our borders and protect the United States from terrorist?

Yes, without a doubt, a President Trump will secure our borders partly by building a fence to keep illegal immigrants, criminals, drug cartels, drugs, and terrorist out of our country. It will be one of his biggest legacies as President to build a border wall and finally do what other Presidents, Democrat and Republican, have not even desired to do, or even thought it was possible to do, since most politicians are alike in that they think inside the box. Mr. Trump takes issues and creates real solutions as if anything is possible in American for the good of we the people. Other politicians recycle old solutions that have never and will never work.

12. Are family and/or friends treating you differently because of your support for Mr. Trump?

My immediate family support me completely in my efforts to help elect Donald Trump as POTUS. They were not surprised in my decision, in fact, they probably respect me more since I was consistent in making my own decision in reference to whom I supported as a presidential candidate whether politically correct to do so or not. One of my friends has openly made fun of Mr. Trump in social media; thus, I decided not to share my choice for candidate as to not influence her in her choices and allowing her the right to freely voice her opinion. As the primary voting day gets closer, I do plan to share my choice for President and explain my rationale for my decision in an effort to sway my friends to consider Mr. Trump.

13. Have you been to a Trump Rally? And if so, would you tell about your experience.

I have not been to a Trump rally as the closest rallies have been hundreds of miles away from my own community since Texas is a large state and Mr. Trump thus far has focused on the larger cities for rallies in Texas.

14. Do you trust Donald J. Trump?

As stated earlier, I most definitely trust Mr. Trump! In fact, when I was deciding on what my twitter handle would be I selected the word "trust"

in my username, @USATrustTrump, to best describe him and it is my number one reason for supporting him. Mr. Trump has it all--the American Dream and beyond. He has a beautiful and devoted family, more money than he and the next few generations of his family will ever need, and he has no other reason to run for President then to make America great again. It is the perfect time in his life cycle to do something to make a massive and pivotal difference in the American people's lives and not just a dent of a change by sponsoring one piece of flimsy legislation in Congress. He will get it done--make America great again. He is the most forthcoming person and transparent person I have ever known who will tell you his view point on any topic. What he utters from his mouth is exactly what he thinks as he does not play the games most people play, and especially the ones politicians play.

15. How will you feel on election day if Donald Trump becomes our President Elect?
I would feel shock and then elation if Mr. Trump wins the Presidency! I would experience a feeling of optimism in that the American Dream would return for the citizenry. I would feel overwhelmed with tears of joy, gratitude, and feel blessed to live in this great country of ours.

16. How will you feel on election day if Donald Trump loses?
A Trump loss would be heartbreaking considering he was the right man for the job and

the only man in my humble opinion. It would be discouraging and somewhat depressing as well as I have come to meet many patriots and individuals on-line on Twitter who put their heart and soul into getting him elected. If a political movement like the one we participated in cannot get our choice of President elected then there is little to no hope that the new President, regardless of who it is, will make the drastic changes in policy that must take place to turn our country around from this self-destructive and downward spiral.

I would feel fearful that within time we would become a third world country as politicians are a changed breed and will do what is politically correct and not what is right and best for its people. The free fall our country is in now would continue leaving me in disbelief and sad for my children and their future.

17. Why do you support Donald J. Trump?

Mr. Trump is a good and moral man and has a proven success track record. The other candidates can only boast about one or two (if any like Mr. Rubio) accomplishments. He is a successful international business man who has earned billions of dollars due to an eye for business and being keen in decision-making. In regards to the million dollar loan his father gave him, well, many children of wealthy parents would have mismanaged the money or not have had as large a success as Mr. Trump. In the America that I know, we do not diminish a person's monumental successes even if family helped along the way. Mr. Trump earned his billions due to his work ethic of working long hours most people would not like to work. America needs to be run like a business to a great extent especially now due to excessive waste in spending and overspending in our federal budget and general mismanagement of government funds. He will make well thought out recommendations to Congress and his cabinet, and staff and transform America with less money taking American into a futuristic 21st century.

Additional Comments by @USATrustTrump:
I was attracted to Mr. Trump and his campaign to be President as we have some personal qualities in common. I have never been politically correct similar to Mr. Trump and people have told me that they come to me when they want honest opinions from someone and not to tell them just what they want to hear. I am also a decisive and passionate person who follows through on any commitment I make. And, perhaps the most important reason for supporting him is that both of us seem to love our country immensely and will do what it takes to make it better.

Another thing that people must know is how some Hispanics, like myself, are baffled that presidential candidates and many Americans believe that we vote Democrat or are for no borders and pro immigration merely because of our heritage. That is a false assumption more than it is a truism. While many times it is true that first generation Hispanics are inclined to vote Democrat, the longer an Hispanic resides in America, adopts the American way of life, and learns about our constitution and that we are the land of opportunity, the more likely that an Hispanic will review their party affiliation and make their own determination based on their values, political party platforms, and other factors. Most people do not know that second and future generations of Hispanics are conservative and a recent Pew Research survey revealed that Hispanics want to restrict immigration.

Ryan F.
Students For Trump

Date: **1/3/2016**
Age: **20, Male**
Lives in **Raleigh, NC**
Party Affiliation: **Republican**
Political Leanings: **Very Conservative**
Ryan voted for in **Mitt Romney in 2012.**

I asked Ryan the following questions and these are his replies, in his own words.

1. What is the first word that comes to mind when you hear the name Donald J. Trump? **Ballsy**

2. What do you consider Trump's strongest personal trait? **Communication**

3. What do you consider Trump's weakest personal trait?
   I am not sure at this given moment.

4. How do you feel about Mr. Trump's family values.
   He loves his family like any other American. Mr. Trump has a work and leisure style relationship with his kids, because they help him run The Trump Organization.

5. Are you concerned with his past marriages and bankruptcies?

No. Mr. Trump is an example of that were are not all perfect individuals. Sometimes you get into relationships and they do not work out. Almost all of us have been in that boat. In regards to Bankruptcies, I believe that it was in his best interest to file bankruptcy to avoid larger loss of company assets.

5. Does it concern you that Mr. Trump was a Democrat before he was a Republican and has donated to both sides?

Like Mr. Trump has said "I like everybody!" From his perspective, I can understand why he would do that. It can be very useful for his business affairs.

6. What concerns you most about the path our country is currently on?

Our economy and the terrible establishment politicians. Both of them put together and you get absolutely no results.

7. What do you expect to see from a Trump Presidency?

I expect to see a boost in our economic status, a "veto" of executive orders made by President Barack Obama and security brought to the American borders.

8. How would a President Trump help your family?

By doing exactly what he says he plans to do. Work out better deals for our country with countries like China, Japan and Iran. He would be

doing a great deal of help to our families by having the border properly secured.

9. Do you think Mr. Trump is straightforward with his plans for the country?

He is very straightforward. He does not beat around the bush like your typical candidate and that is why many people love him.

10. In your opinion, would a President Trump secure our borders and protect the United States from terrorist?

Yes, of course. If our military has increased spending with more troops, that is a large step already. Our current president decreased DOD budgets and with that, our military size has decreased. I believe that if we increase defense spending, add more border security and of course, build a new border wall, then we will be a lot better off than we are now.

11. Are family and/or friends treating you differently because of your support for Mr. Trump?

No, my family is of course on board. Some friends have commented and stated they do not like Trump because of some of his comments, but they also said they were not ruling out the possibility of voting for him.

12. Have you been to a Trump Rally? And if so, would you tell about your experience.

Yes, I have been to one Trump Rally in Raleigh, NC. I was there behind the scenes as I am the

National Chairman of Students for Trump. It was a once in a lifetime feeling. There were thousands of people cramped into one building and the capacity was met. It is just amazing to look around the room from the press stage and see the faces of all these people and how they light up when Trump takes the stage. The amount of enthusiasm and roar that comes from the crowd is mesmerizing to say the least.

13. Do you trust Donald J. Trump?

Yes, I do. He has come this far, risking his business and all of his assets to tell the American people how it should be done and how he is going to get it done if elected.

13. How will you feel on election day if Donald Trump becomes our President Elect?

I will feel as if I succeeded in helping him getting elected.

14. How will you feel on election day if Donald Trump loses?

What we do in supporting the campaign is hard work. It takes a lot of time and effort. But in the end, we understand that losing is a possibility that is never narrowed out, no matter how successful you may be in the campaign running. He could lose and if he does, I will be content knowing he made it this far and he started conversations that would of never happened.

15. Why do you support Donald J. Trump?

I support Donald J. Trump for President of the United States because his love for this country. Like I said before, he has risked so much to get on that stage and tell the American people like it is. Many people get upset, but a lot more clap in appreciation and love for him doing it. I support him because he represents a breed of politicians that we have not seen in many years. Politicians that are not afraid to speak their minds and get the job done by doing the right thing and not the Politically Correct one.

CATHERINE F.

Date: **January 2, 2016**
Age: **59, Female**
Lives in **Pleasantville, NJ**
Party Affiliation: **Democrat**
Political Leanings: **Lean Conservative**
Catherine voted for **President Barack Obama in 2012.**

1. What is the first word that comes to mind when you hear the name Donald J. Trump?
   Excitement!

2. What do you consider Trump's strongest personal trait? **Strong leadership.**

3. What do you consider Trump's weakest personal trait? **Redundant**

4. How do you feel about Mr. Trump's family values?
   He is fiercely loyal to those he loves.

5. Are you concerned with his past marriages and bankruptcies?   **NO**

6. Does it concern you that Mr. Trump was a Democrat before he was a Republican and has donated to both sides?
   Not at all.

7. What concerns you most about the path our country is currently on?

America is starting down a path of losing her sovereignty through one-sided trade deals, New World Order politics run by wealthy individuals and corporations, bought and paid for politicians who only want to enrich themselves, open-border policies, and stagnant wages.

8. What do you expect to see from a Trump Presidency?

Return of manufacturing and jobs, national security in the form of a wall on our southern border coupled with greater screening for those entering the US, improvements in infrastructure, lower taxes, ending the wars in the Middle East and improve America's standing in the world.

9. How would a President Trump help your family?

Providing lower taxes, preserving SS and Medicare, improving roads, bridges and airports, and bringing peace and prosperity back to the US.

10. Do you think Mr. Trump is straightforward with his plans for the country? **Absolutely, yes!**

11. In your opinion, would a President Trump secure our borders and protect the United States from terrorist?

Absolutely, yes...Donald Trump is the best person to take on this challenge. We need strong leadership!

12. Are family and/or friends treating you differently because of your support for Mr. Trump?

Yes, some people who don't really understand him. Others are surprisingly supportive and a few have changed from Democrat to Republican just to vote for Trump.

13. Have you been to a Trump Rally? And if so, would you tell about your experience.   **No.**

14. Do you trust Donald J. Trump? **Yes**

15. How will you feel on election day if Donald Trump becomes our President Elect?

Ecstatic and hopeful for my family and my country.

16. How will you feel on election day if Donald Trump loses?   **Angry, sad and hopeless.**

17. Why do you support Donald J. Trump?

He's the best candidate out there to make a positive change in our country in many different ways.

PEGGY_6824

Peggy, who prefers to go only by her on-line avatar, peggy_6824, wrote this in her words instead of using the survey form. She say:

"AS AN AMERICAN CITIZEN OF LATIN/HISPANIC DESCENT WHOSE FIRST LANGUAGE IS SPANISH, I am glad to see the American people finally waking up to the fact that; the "American Dream" is now defined as cradle to grave/generational support at the expense of the American people. Their version of the "American Dream" is one in which their "American Dreams" are financed by the American people.

The American people from all walks of life are coming together and coalescing behind Donald Trump and Ted Cruz for the following reasons because it negatively impacts all of us regardless of race and demographics;

THE AMERICAN PEOPLE ARE TIRED OF BEING TREATED AS A FORCED CHARITY VIA INCREASED TAXES TO PAY FOR EVERY UNEDUCATED AND IMPOVERISHED PERSON AND THEIR FAMILIES WHO ENTER THE COUNTRY EITHER LEGALLY AS A SUPPOSED REFUGEES OR ILLEGALLY BECAUSE THEY ARE ALL BASICALLY NOTHING BUT ECONOMIC MIGRANTS. THEY ALL COME IN SEARCH OF THEIR "AMERICAN DREAM" FINANCED BY THE AMERICAN PEOPLE/TAXPAYERS VIA WELFARE, FOOD STAMPS, FREE EDUCATIONS, FREE HEALTH

CARE, SOCIAL SECURITY THEY DID NOT EARN, FREE HOUSING, FREE OBAMA-PHONES, ETC. THIS SEEMS TO BE NOT ONLY A LIFETIME PROPOSITION BUT A GENERATIONAL PROPOSITION!!!!!

In return we get;

• Increased unemployment for American citizens.

• Our identities/social security numbers stolen.

• Reduced wages.

• Overcrowded schools.

• The resurgence of diseases that were long ago eradicated that are killing our children.

• Increase of illicit/deadly drugs that are killing American citizens.

• Overburdened/bankrupt hospitals.

• Disenfranchisement of the right as illegals cast fraudulent votes which skew our elections.

• Increased crime.

• Overcrowded jails/prisons.

• 340 sanctuary cities across the US created by Democrats and funded by the Republican RINOs.

• The release of thousands of murderers, rapists, & pedophiles into our communities to commit even more crimes.

• Terrorists entering the US thanks to Obama and his administration's non-existent immigration enforcement and refusal to secure our borders and tourist visa programs.

Democrats get;

• An expanded voter base paid for by the American people/taxpayers.

Establishment Republicans/RINOs like Marco Rubio, Jeb Bush, John Kasich, etc. get;

• To line their pockets with more money from the donor class a.k.a. special interests, big labor, & the Chamber of Commerce who seek cheap labor for whom they do not need to provide health insurance per Obamacare making it a win-win for them while the American people are forced to subsidize their cheap labor.

Thanks to Obama, the Democrats, and the RINOs;

They along with our own elected representatives are destroying our taxpayer funded safety net intended for our own citizens and threaten to bankrupt our nation. Our own elderly, vets, truly disabled, handicapped, and poor are being robbed.

Who exactly were they elected to represent????

The American people are the most charitable people in the world but we have to draw the line when we are being forcibly enslaved for the benefit of others.

Let's not forget how many of our own citizens are unemployed and homeless while Obama and both Democrats and Republicans seek to increase our taxes to support hundreds of thousands from other countries and put their needs above those of American citizens.

With regard to being called racists, bigots, white supremacists, etc.! Been there, done that with the POS in the White House and many bought into it and the guilt that went with it and look where we are now!

As an American citizen of Hispanic descent whose first language is Spanish and a minority, I absolutely know with 100% certainty that this is not about not being a welcoming nation, hatred, bigotry, racism, xenophobia, discrimination, being nativists, anti-Immigrant, or Anti-Hispanic and like Ted Cruz, I too find such accusations offensive! This is about the economic survival of our nation/citizenry. Thus we are absolutely anti- parasite, moocher, leech, sponger, bloodsucker, freeloader, etc.

For millions of American citizens of Latino/Hispanic descent this is about, honor, integrity, morals, values, self-respect, and our belief in the rule of law and that the US is a sovereign nation and that supersedes shared blood, ancestry, and heritage, thus to suggest that we would even consider abandoning those very values and beliefs ingrained in us to support millions of illegal's is an insult of epic proportions.

Better Trump or Cruz than those we absolutely know will continue Obama's policies of mass immigration that will destroy the US and the American people/taxpayers!

These so called "immigrants" have nothing in common with the immigrants of yesteryear who came in search of the "American Dream" that they knew could only be achieved through their own ingenuity and hard work. Those were their expectations. They did not come looking to be supported by their fellow Americans!

TRUMP/CRUZ 2016

JACOB

Date: **1/2/2016**
Age: **30, Male**
Lives in **Brooklyn, NY**
Level of Education: **College**
Party Affiliation: **Independent**
Political Leanings: **Conservative**
Jacob **did not** vote in 2012.

1. What is the first word that comes to mind when you hear the name Donald J. Trump?
Driven

2. What do you consider Trump's strongest personal trait?
Boldness. He has tremendous goals in all that he sets out to accomplish, whether it's a business opportunity, a deal, a relationship, a project etc, and and an even more tremendous will to see those goals realized - quickly, efficiently, and beautifully.

He approaches his objectives with a very unusual sense of drive and motivation which carry through and breed stunning success.

This same theme is taking place now during his most recent entry into politics. Mediocre just isn't an option, and he is not just another candidate.

3. What do you consider Trump's weakest personal trait?
Humility. He has obviously been at the executive position for most of his life, and that's where he has

found his place and is comfortable. You can see that he thinks like an executive and approaches everything from a controlling position, rather than a navigating position.

While this is really what is needed to be an effective company leader, it does make a person less receptive to advice and less capable of accommodation.

In American politics, you are not the boss. You are elected and are technically employed by the people of the country. What they say and think of you matters. It is NOT your private business in which you can be a dictator. You have to do what THEY want, and if they're not happy, your job and success are on the line.

Additionally, there's congress and the house to deal with. Even if you have a very effective plan, unless the lawmakers are on board it won't go anywhere.

I think this will be his greatest difficulty in office.

4. How do you feel about Mr. Trump's family values.

While I am more traditional and less materialistic myself, he is certainly a man with positive and healthy family values.

5. Are you concerned with his past marriages and bankruptcies?

In terms of the marriages, he probably could have balanced his focus between business and family a little better, but his business meant everything to him and he sacrificed everything for it. I would be more concerned with someone who had no life and had been through three marriages.

The bankruptcies were handled very well and he made a strong comeback. Essentially a business loan is a bank trying to make money by lending it to a company to conduct business. There is always the understanding that there is a risk involved. I don't think any of the deals that went bad were irresponsible or badly thought out, they were deals that should have worked but didn't.

6. Does it concern you that Mr. Trump was a Democrat before he was a Republican and has donated to both sides?

One of the aspects to Mr. Trump's appeal is his commitment to common sense and distance from ideology in general. A democrat out of convenience and practicality is very different than a democrat due to ideology. Life comes with experience and experience changes people's opinions.

Let's approach the question from the angle which people (ie: Rand Paul) are concerned about. Is Donald Trump a "fake conservative"? Meaning, is he expressing views and opinions which he himself does not actually believe, only to garner support from the republican electorate. To be completely honest, I do not believe that Donald Trump would be much different in word and policy if he ran as a democrat. As it is, he is more of a centrist than either democrat or republican.

The area which makes him appear very much on the republican side are his hawkish views on foreign policy and crime. He is VERY far from a liberal or anything like it. Like I said, he is coming from a very practical common sense point of view, and that runs parallel to republican/conservative thought most of the time.

I think it's a plus that he was able to work with everybody he needed to for his business. Only a republican through ideology would abstain from donating to democrats despite the business gains which would be achieved by doing so.

7. What concerns you most about the path our country is currently on?

We are a country which is rapidly losing its sense of identity. All the things which we used to identify ourselves with and ascribe meaning with have been blanket labeled by the left as either racist, bigoted, homophobic, xenophobic, or generally fear related.

People have largely lost the drive to prosper, and we are watching a national decline in motion. The economy has been run and regulated by lawmakers looking to line their pockets at the expense of every working family in the country, and the corruption is taking a huge toll on everyone.

There is an epic failure happening with regard to recognizing the threats we face and their true sources and breeding grounds.

8. What do you expect to see from a Trump Presidency?

I expect efficiency and success in 5 main categories:

1) **National security**
2) **Trade**
3) **Economic growth/jobs**
4) **Immigration**
5) **Normalization of domestic social policy**

Additionally, I believe there a numerous other areas which will flourish under Trump, such as infrastructure, US manufacturing + exports, health-care, army vet care, and scientific research and development.

9. How would a President Trump help your family?

Every family living in the US will be better off with a safer, wealthier, stronger, happier, more productive nation around them.

10. Do you think Mr. Trump is straightforward with his plans for the country?

Yes. Like every politician he does have to navigate his way around the media to make his points, as they have agendas and their questions and discussions almost always are aimed at hurting him rather than bringing the viewers the truth of what he's saying, but for the most part he is being truthful about what he wants to do and what he's going to do.

11. In your opinion, would a President Trump secure our borders and protect the United States from terrorist?

Absolutely! It was the first thing he spoke about and has been a central theme of his throughout his campaign. Border security is vital for the economy,

but since 9-11 it has become a life and death issue as well. The reason other politicians look away from it is for one reason and one reason only: donors.

One of the greatest elements to Trumps appeal is his lack of obligations to corporations. He has no reason to run the US according to THEIR needs and can instead focus on the needs of the people.

12. Are family and/or friends treating you differently because of your support for Mr. Trump?

No, but his brashness does scare some people. His honesty and no-nonsense common sense approach is not unusual from a regular person, but you NEVER hear someone speaking that way in public, certainly not a politician.

Political correctness has effectively silenced the majority of the United States of America, and here you have an individual who's not having any of it.

Admittedly, he is not polished and has a rather uncouth manner of expressing himself. I pride myself in being able to focus on content rather than delivery and externals.

This is not Xbox, we can't design our own candidate. If I could, I guess I would set the "polished" marker on 10 instead of 4 but that is how you deal with fantasy. In real life you have real choices to make, and you only have the cards you're dealt. Anyone who truly loves his family and values his life will be able to look past silly external sentiment and see what's truly behind each candidate.

That being said, claims that he is a racist are 100% false. Anyone who takes the time to examine the statements and look up the definition of "racist" will see the dis-ingenuity of these claims. The left has rewritten the dictionary and is labeling any threat to their political power as racist. It's a lie.

13. Have you been to a Trump Rally? And if so, would you tell about your experience.

I have not, but by the looks of them I would love to experience one first hand.

14. Do you trust Donald J. Trump?

I trust him to take his job and commander in chief seriously and to fix most of the major problems threatening the country.

15. How will you feel on election day if Donald Trump becomes our President Elect?

I will not be surprised but it will be a very relieved and liberating feeling. This country has been in careless, dishonest, incompetent, and thieving hands for way too long. We are not in great shape.

16. How will you feel on election day if Donald Trump loses?

Very let down, like we blew our one chance to be in good hands.

17. Why do you support Donald J. Trump?

I'm all about the numbers and results. I love my children and it's not enough for me that society doesn't collapse tomorrow. I don't want my kids to ever witness killing in the streets or political havoc. Not now, not in 30 years. So when I look at Donald, I see someone who will set the country right in a very practical way and create a new leadership status quo of common sense and responsibility.

CAROLINE M.

Date: **1/15/16**
Age: **73, Female**
Level of Education: **College**
Lives in **Setauket, NY**
Party Affiliation: **Republican**
Caroline voted for **Mitt Romney in 2012.**

1. What is the first word that comes to mind when you hear the name Donald J. Trump?   **Truth**

2. What do you consider Trump's strongest personal trait?   **Stamina**

3. What do you consider Trump's weakest personal trait? **NONE**

4. How do you feel about Mr. Trump's family values? **LOVE THEM**

5. Are you concerned with his past marriages and bankruptcies? **NO**

6. Does it concern you that Mr. Trump was a Democrat before he was a Republican and has donated to both sides? **NO**

7. What concerns you most about the path our country is currently on?   **The Media Lies**

8. What do you expect to see from a Trump Presidency?   **Sweeping reforms.**

9. How would a President Trump help your family? **Owes no favors.**

10. Do you think Mr. Trump is straightforward with his plans for the country?
    Straight-forward? The best candidate in my lifetime.

11. In your opinion, would a President Trump secure our borders and protect the United States from terrorist? **YES**

12. Are family and/or friends treating you differently because of your support for Mr. Trump? **YES**

13. Have you been to a Trump Rally? And if so, would you tell about your experience. **YES**

14. Do you trust Donald J. Trump? **YES**

15. How will you feel on election day if Donald Trump becomes our President Elect? **Ecstatic**

16. How will you feel on election day if Donald Trump loses? **America loses - America is done!**

17. Why do you support Donald J. Trump?
    We need a doer in the White House. When Mr. Trump says he is going to do it. It gets done! I'm a

NY'er and have followed Him for years! He is the real deal - America needs him, no more lies,-no more do nothing politicians. I will vote for Donald Trump. Get this - his supporters are loyal and LOVE him!

JERRY B.

Jerry B. is a 56 yr old carpenter from Valley Center, Kansas, just outside of Wichita.

Although he never worked directly for Mr. Trump, he has worked on projects for contractors who knew of Mr. Trump's reputation as far back as the early 90's. Jerry witnessed tremendous respect for Trump's business abilities by everyone in the industry.

Jerry went on to own his own company building McDonald's, KFCs, Pizza Huts, and prisons. In his 40 years as a contractor, he's traveled the United States and has lived a pretty exciting life.

He lost his business after being seriously injured and now he calls himself a "worn-out old carpenter, who lives in cold Kansas" and he really wants Donald Trump for President.

Feeling depressed, unable to support his family the way he was used to doing, he now works part-time restoring old houses and hopes someday to be able to rebuild his crippled construction company.

Government regulations are a big hurdle for him right now. Unable to afford things like Workers Compensation Insurance, General Liability Insurance, Business license, fees and permits, Obama Care Insurance, Payroll taxes, on and on. Small construction companies, like he used to have, are bombarded with new regulations, fees, and taxes, making it impossible for someone like Jerry to afford running their own businesses now.

It's cheaper for him to just to work on old houses and sell them but he hopes that when Mr. Trump becomes President Trump, he will get rid of some of those harmful regulations, fire the IRS, run off the special interest groups and lobbyist, and then loan him enough start-up money to open another construction company.

All Jerry wants is the opportunity to "rebuild America" by criss-crossing the nation fixing up old run-down restaurants. He imagines families and couples sitting down in a fresh new American restaurant, look around, and see a bright, shiny penny and not the tarnished remnants of neglect.

He wants people to take pride in their country once again and he wants everyone to know that it's people like him, Americans who want to work, that re-built a beautiful America.

"Jerry Loses Hope"

Since the 2008 election of President Obama, Jerry would turn on the TV and watch Fox News debate over how bad Obama was turning out to be.

Like me, he kept hoping to hear that Donald Trump was going to run and when he didn't run in 2012, Jerry became despondent, believing the country would never get out of this mess.

He decided that if Trump ever did run, he would try to help him win. On June 16, 2015, when like the rest of us, he heard the news, he knew he had to make good on his promise to help Mr. Trump win.

Social Media was a huge part of Barack Obama's ground game. The future President was young and savvy in the ways of the Internet and he employed a campaign staff who knew how to use Social Media to their benefit, giving him the edge needed to wipe the floor with his competition.

Getting involved in Social Media seemed like a waste of time to Jerry as he'd rather be building a piece of furniture in his wood-working shop or restore an old house as opposed to messing with Facebook or Twitter.

But then came his injury, followed by surgery and all of the sudden, he had tremendous time on his hands. He watched more and more Fox News and spent time visiting his brother in Florida.

He and David would talk about everything; from cars to building projects and even politics. They talked about Obama, Hillary Clinton and Harry Reid and about the betrayal of both parties. They got angry over the politicians always bowing to the whims of the lobbyist, donors and special interest groups. They felt, like most people, that the politicians were destroying our once great country.

His talks with his wise, older brother made the small spark of anger they were both feeling, grow strong and bright.

So he eventually jumped on the Social Media bandwagon, opening a Pro-Trump Twitter page and today he has over 2700 Twitter followers. He works hard to keep his followers informed of "anything Trump" especially dispelling the lies.

Jerry says he's always looked up to Mr. Trump and has great respect for Trumps capabilities. Jerry says, "Trump has built amazing structure's, some of them the most desired in the world. Being in construction myself, I know firsthand what goes into building the kinds of things that Donald Trump builds. That's how I know Mr. Trump's reputation is strong."

When he heard Trump announce he was running for President he was very happy and wanted to be a part of the Trump Team. So braving the Internet again, he signed up to be a volunteer on Donald Trump's website.

Being partially disabled he couldn't really attend a rally or leave the house to volunteer, so he threw himself into Twitter working hours a day building a network of followers he could use to help spread the word about Donald Trump. Jerry Brown felt very strongly that if Donald Trump could give up his lifestyle in order to campaign, then he could do his small part by getting the word out to as many as possible through his Twitter account.

Jerry fights the trolls on-line when they spout lies about his hero because getting out the truth is his way of helping Mr. Trump in the fight to make our country great again.

So many people just like Jerry believe in truth, honesty, justice, and especially, they believe in the spirit of America.

Jerry Brown, from Kansas, says "Mr. Trump is from my world and he wants to remodel our America, put it back, only better than it was before. I know his kind, they have to get it right. Donald Trump will get it right."

Mr. Brown wants everyone to dream about the future once more and have hope of better times and he firmly believes that Donald J. Trump is the man for not only him, but for all of America.

DALLAS H.

Date: **1/29/16**
Age: **30, Male**
Lives in **Orlando, Florida**
Level of Education: **Some college**
Party Affiliation:
Libertarian except that they support open borders. Republican to vote for Trump. Ex-Democrat.
  Dallas voted for **"Anti- American Tyrant Obama" in 2012.**

1. What is the first word that comes to mind when you hear the name Donald J. Trump? **Winner**

2. What do you consider Trump's strongest personal trait? **Fearless**

3. What do you consider Trump's weakest personal trait? **To brash. Maybe needs to tone it down ever so slightly. He is an ego maniac but that could be a good thing because he is driven to succeed and as President if he succeeds then the American people succeed.**

4. How do you feel about Mr. Trump's family values? **He has raised a great family. That shows how he is as a leader. A lot of rich kids grow up to be spoiled brats.**

5. Are you concerned with his past marriages and bankruptcies?

No and no. The left and some Republicans even use the bankruptcy thing to attack Trump because they know the average leftist has no idea about bankruptcy law. Bankruptcy is an absolutely crucial aspect of capitalism and finance. There would be no big business, small business, hotels, theme parks, restaurants, big box stores, innovation or anything at all without bankruptcy law. Without bankruptcy there is no capitalism. The banks know all about bankruptcy when they agree to lend that money. They win some and they lose some but that is how business works. So the whole bankruptcy issue is really insulting to my intelligence. By the way, this country is essentially bankrupt and I want a strong leader like Trump who will negotiate with our creditors and make sure we get a great deal so that we don't have to live under crushing austerity like Greece and other countries that have been decimated by big banks. I don't believe trump will allow our creditors to destroy this nation. So actually the fact that trump has gone through bankruptcy is a good thing.

6. Does it concern you that Mr. Trump was a Democrat before he was a Republican and has donated to both sides? **Not at all. I was a registered democrat until recently. Not that I ever supported Democrat policies; it's just I did not really follow politics and always thought the Democrats were the good guys because I would watch Jon Stewart and Colbert and they do a great job of spinning and deceiving just like the rest of the media including Fox news. But shortly after 2012 I started really learning**

about politics. I have learned so much in the last three years about the founding fathers, the Constitution, liberty, limited government, the free market, etc. Now I despise Obama and Hillary Clinton. But I also despise the republican establishment because they are a bunch of scum as well. I like that Trump is rich, powerful, fearless and willing to take on both sides of the corrupt establishment because that is what we need.

7. What concerns you most about the path our country is currently on? **Where do we start? First of the economy. We cannot keep sending our jobs to communist nations such as China and Vietnam. The Republicans and Democrats tell us "free trade" is good for American workers but when I see thousands of factories shut down and once prospering cities turned into third world slums I know there is a problem. I am for trade but we need fair trade that benefits America. Not crony capitalist trade where we send our factories overseas to exploit cheap slave labor. We should not be collaborating with the Communist Party of China to exploit their slave labor while Americans are put out of a job. Also there is war. The establishment Republicans and democrats seem to want war with Russia. They talk about stopping Iran from getting a nuclear bomb but Russia already has thousands! Trump is the only one who wants to get along with Putin and that is a big deal. there is no greater threat to humanity than nuclear war. We should never back down to Russia but at the same time we should not be provoking Russia.**

Also, the establishment Democrats and Republicans have destroyed the Middle East with these insane democracy projects. Those people do not understand democracy and are not ready for freedom. The Middle East is an extremely volatile region that requires strongmen and dictators to keep the people in line. Remove the dictators and the Jihadist are free to run rampant committing mass murder and atrocities. Trump was against the Iraq war because he is brilliant and thinks ahead. The Democrat and Republican establishment are responsible for creating mass chaos but they are still in power and that is insane. Anybody who voted for the Iraq war should be banned from public office for life, not running for President like Hillary Clinton. Also, we must lower taxes. The Democrats want to raise taxes to 45% so they can give free college and health-care to everybody from the third world who can make it here. They are trying to bankrupt us! So that leads me to immigration. I am not against immigrants. I love them. I love diversity. I know so many people from different countries including the Middle East and they are all great people but at the same time we simply must control our borders and let in who we want and who will benefit us. You can't even rent a cheap apartment without passing a background check and most apartments are gated so why is it wrong to put a fence around the country and vet who comes in?

8. What do you expect to see from a Trump Presidency? **I expect to see a man of the people**

making good decisions on behalf of Americans
rather than on behalf of lobbyists.

9. How would a President Trump help your family?
**He won't let in people from the Middle East who
want to kill us. he won't start WWIII with Russia.
He will convince congress to lower taxes which will
allow us to keep more money. He will oversee better
trade deals so hopefully Americans can get to work
again. He will convince congress to build the wall so
that we have control over who comes here and who
does not.**

10. Do you think Mr. Trump is straightforward
with his plans for the country? **Absolutely! The
media says Trump has no substance but that is
because they are a bunch of deceptive scum. trump
has policy busting out his socks. His vision is
perfectly clear.**

11. In your opinion, would a President Trump
secure our borders and protect the United States from
terrorist? **YES !!!!**

12. Are family and/or friends treating you
differently because of your support for Mr. Trump?
**Very few. I know some ignorant Hillary
Supporters. But almost everybody I talk to
including Democrats support Trump. Even people
who don't only take a quick conversation to get
them to see where Trump is coming from. I was in
a class for international real estate which was
extremely diverse and there was a consensus that**

trump was the man for the job. A Hispanic man stood up and proclaimed "I can't stand Donald trump but he is the right man for the job." Almost all Spanish people I know support Trump.

13. Have you been to a Trump Rally? And if so, would you tell about your experience. **I have watched several on-line. Trump is a showman. He gives the people what they want.**

14. Do you trust Donald J. Trump? **Yes, but if he crosses the American people then I will support impeaching him. We still have checks and balances. I have no unconditional loyalty. I support Trump as long as he supports the people. I trust that he will do what's right.**

15. How will you feel on election day if Donald Trump becomes our President Elect? **I will feel great. Trump is just one man and he can't fix things by himself or overnight but good leadership is crucial. Like a football team, sometime the team has amazing talent but the head coach is just not getting the job done so they fire the head coach and if they hire the right new head coach the team can go to the super bowl the next year. America has the talent. All we need is a good head coach like Trump who loves America, loves to win, knows how to win, refuses to loose, refuses to back down, is fearless, is a great leader and will be a great motivator.**

16. How will you feel on election day if Donald Trump loses? **Very depressed. I have talked to**

people who said if Hillary wins they will move, although I don't know where because the leftists are destroying Europe. I think America will find a way to become great again regardless but I think trump would be a great help.

17. Why do you support Donald J. Trump?

YES, I could talk trump and politics all day. I hope your book turns out good. I look forward to reading it.

SHELLEY

Date: **2/21/2016**
Age: **47, Female**
Lives in **Dacula, GA**
Level of Education: **Master of Education**
Party Affiliation: **Republican**
Shelley **chose not to vote** in 2012.

1. What is the first word that comes to mind when you hear the name Donald J. Trump? **Passion**

2. What do you consider Trump's strongest personal trait? **Connects with the middle class working people.**

3. What do you consider Trump's weakest personal trait? **Needs to calm down a bit when attacking people. I don't mind the attack but Trump takes it to the next level and I worry how the media will twist it.**

4. How do you feel about Mr. Trump's family values? **Strong; raised 3 successful adults and 1 in college-- doing something right! His kids are out of the tabloids and such unlike other wealthy families. I am sure Barron will be just as successful!**

5. Are you concerned with his past marriages and bankruptcies? **Not one bit!**

6. Does it concern you that Mr. Trump was a Democrat before he was a Republican and has donated

to both sides? **No! I grew up in a democratic house and I am Republican. Democrats have drastically changed over the years, and many have gone to the Right.**

7. What concerns you most about the path our country is currently on? **National security and increase of refugees/ Islamic people. Give it a few generations and it will totally change the demographics of this country.**

8. What do you expect to see from a Trump Presidency? **Leadership!!!!**

9. How would a President Trump help your family? **National security. I have an 18 year old son and the last thing I want is to see a draft because we don't have strong leadership. My beautiful daughter is 12.5 years old and her safety is #1!!! Trump, secure our borders and keep refugees out!**

10. Do you think Mr. Trump is straightforward with his plans for the country? **Yes and people need to understand he does not need to "show his hand"! Cruz is already copying some of his ideas and verbiage!**

11. In your opinion, would a President Trump secure our borders and protect the United States from terrorist? **Yes very much so. I think other countries are shaking in their pants that the silent majority has spoken!**

12. Are family and/or friends treating you differently because of your support for Mr. Trump? **No.**

13. Have you been to a Trump Rally? And if so, would you tell about your experience. **I've been to two rallies; both awesome -front row! Well worth the long wait! I love Trump!**

14. Do you trust Donald J. Trump? **Absolutely! He loves America and her people!**

15. How will you feel on election day if Donald Trump becomes our President Elect? **Awesome! Mission successful!**

16. How will you feel on election day if Donald Trump loses? **Worried for my children's future.**

When you get a moment, please visit Shelley's Facebook page at: WomenforTrump

LORI H.

Date: **1/8/2016**
Age: **43, Female**
Lives in **Claremont, NH**
Level of Education: **12+**
Party Affiliation: **Republican**
Voted for in 2012? **I don't remember.... BUT IT WASN'T OBAMA!!!!!!**

1. What is the first word that comes to mind when you hear the name Donald J. Trump? **Strong**

2. What do you consider Trump's strongest personal trait? **Financially intelligent.**

3. What do you consider Trump's weakest personal trait? **The fact that he has millions...I think a lot of people just see him as WEALTHY and not see how intelligent he is and how he got to be WHO he is and WHERE he is.**

4. How do you feel about Mr. Trump's family values? **I think he has strong family values that will influence his actions as President and as a result, protect us as a nation.**

5. Are you concerned with his past marriages and bankruptcies? **Not at all, I think it makes him "one of us", which is why we relate to him.**

6. Does it concern you that Mr. Trump was a Democrat before he was a Republican and has donated

to both sides? **No it just means that he has experienced both sides of all the issues.**

7. What concerns you most about the path our country is currently on? **This country has gone to hell and Trump is gonna bring it back...this country is on the brink of a civil war and financial ruin.**

8. What do you expect to see from a Trump Presidency?
A financially stable country, less crime...healthier veterans...job opportunities...our companies coming back and all around happier people.

9. How would a President Trump help your family? **More affordable health care and jobs.**

10. Do you think Mr. Trump is straightforward with his plans for the country? **Yes...I don't think he holds anything back, which is why he can be trusted.**

11. In your opinion, would a President Trump secure our borders and protect the United States from terrorist? **I absolutely believe he is going to build a wall (and Mexico IS gonna pay it) and he is going to remove our threat and fear of terrorists.**

12. Are family and/or friends treating you differently because of your support for Mr. Trump? **Absolutely, but it will never change my opinions or**

beliefs and I believe **Trump is the man who is
finally going to fix this country.**

13. Have you been to a Trump Rally? And if so,
would you tell about your experience. **Yes I have been
to a rally...I thought it was enjoyable, he is a
wonderful speaker, he can hold your attention and
loves to make jokes and laugh but still firmly states
his plans and promises. He speaks to the people in a
way the people can understand. He doesn't use big
words and phrases that mean nothing to the
average person.**

14. Do you trust Donald J. Trump? **Yes I do. That
is why I praise him and I refuse to listen to the
protesters.**

15. How will you feel on election day if Donald
Trump becomes our President Elect? **RELIEVED**

16. How will you feel on election day if Donald
Trump loses?
**I will feel like all is lost for this country...if we
keep going down this highway to hell, we will never
be able to return no matter how good the GPS is....I
don't think this country can survive another 4
years without Trump.**

17. Additional Comments:
**WHEN Trump wins we can finally stand up and
shout "we are proud to be in America" and thank
him for making this a safe and happy place again.**

DEAN W.

Date: **1/7/2016**
Age: **60, Male**
Lives in **Tiskilwa, Illinois**
Level of Education: **HS (also Paralegal)**
Party Affiliation: **Independent**
Dean **begrudgingly voted for Mitt Romney** in 2012.

1. What is the first word that comes to mind when you hear the name Donald J. Trump? **Potential**

2. What do you consider Trump's strongest personal trait? **Proven economic/business success.**

3. What do you consider Trump's weakest personal trait? **His false start campaign last cycle.**

4. How do you feel about Mr. Trump's family values? **Outstanding, functioning family. All family members tremendous role models.**

5. Are you concerned with his past marriages and bankruptcies? **To a small degree, but they seem to be generally benign in nature.**

6. Does it concern you that Mr. Trump was a Democrat before he was a Republican and has donated to both sides? **No, my concern is with both parties, and the political corruption on both sides.**

7. What concerns you most about the path our country is currently on? **Political corruption, federal and global overreach.**

8. What do you expect to see from a Trump Presidency? **Great increase of personal American wealth, streamlined government, border and national security.**

9. How would a President Trump help your family? **By securing and enriching America and Citizens first.**

10. Do you think Mr. Trump is straightforward with his plans for the country? **Generally yes, but it seems to me he plays a lot by ear. If he is true to his implied loyalty to America and Citizens, then that works for me.**

11. In your opinion, would a President Trump secure our borders and protect the United States from terrorist? **I really think so, and do believe he can and will charge Mexico for building the southern wall. And his experience of vetting the right people for the right jobs will make for outstanding cabinet appointments.**

12. Are family and/or friends treating you differently because of your support for Mr. Trump? They have a**ll have lost their thrill of hope and change, I just don't rub it in.**

13. Have you been to a Trump Rally? And if so, would you tell about your experience. **Not in person, have watched most live or soon after. Tremendous crowds with positive energy. Refreshing.**

14. Do you trust Donald J. Trump? **The $64,000 question. The future cannot be predicted, but yes, if he is true to his word, he has the greatest potential to do the greatest good of all the 2016 candidates.**

15. How will you feel on election day if Donald Trump becomes our President Elect? **Relieved, cautiously optimistic.**

16. How will you feel on election day if Donald Trump loses?
If by Cruz, then a lot, but not all is lost. If by anyone else, then more of the same as last 8 years, leading to great civil unrest, potentially war.

Additional Comments:
I am a soon to retired veteran. Thank-you for the support of Mr. Trump and America.

JAN P.

Date: **2/21/2016**
Age: **65, Female**
Lives in **Yucaipa, California**
Level of Education: **Some College**
Party Affiliation: **Republican**
Jan voted for **President Barack Obama** in 2012

1.   What is the first word that comes to mind
       when you hear the name Donald J. Trump?
       Real.

2. What do you consider Trump's strongest
personal trait? **The way he speaks, he's a breath of
fresh air!**

3. What do you consider Trump's weakest personal
trait? **He doesn't have one.**

4. How do you feel about Mr. Trump's family
values? **Wonderful!**

5. Are you concerned with his past marriages and
bankruptcies? **NO!**

6. Does it concern you that Mr. Trump was a
Democrat before he was a Republican and has donated
to both sides? **No.**

7. What concerns you most about the path our
country is currently on?
       It's going down the toilet.

8. What do you expect to see from a Trump Presidency? **A much better way of life fair to all.**

9. How would a President Trump help your family? **In a lot of ways!!!**

10. Do you think Mr. Trump is straightforward with his plans for the country? **Yes.**

11. In your opinion, would a President Trump secure our borders and protect the United States from terrorist? **Yes.**

12. Are family and/or friends treating you differently because of your support for Mr. Trump? **No and I wouldn't care anyway.**

13. Have you been to a Trump Rally? And if so, would you tell about your experience.
No I have not.

14. Do you trust Donald J. Trump? **Yes.**

15. How will you feel on election day if Donald Trump becomes our President Elect?
Wonderful !!!

16. How will you feel on election day if Donald Trump loses?
Horrible !!!

Additional Comments:

Mr. Trump is a breath of fresh air and we need someone like him to get this country back to what it was.

JENNETT P.

Date: **1/8/2016**
Age: **70, Female**
Lives in **Pelham, Alabama**
Level of Education: **3 yrs of college**
Party Affiliation: **Independent**
Political Leanings:
Jennett voted for **Mitt Romney in 2012.**

1. What is the first word that comes to mind when you hear the name Donald J. Trump? **Competent**

2. What do you consider Trump's strongest personal trait? **Leadership**

3. What do you consider Trump's weakest personal trait? **Says what he thinks.**

4. How do you feel about Mr. Trump's family values? **Good**

5. Are you concerned with his past marriages and bankruptcies?   **NO**

6. Does it concern you that Mr. Trump was a Democrat before he was a Republican and has donated to both sides? **No - I voted democrat once, too.**

7. What concerns you most about the path our country is currently on? **Islam, terrorism, debt, loose moral values - not necessarily in that order.**

8. What do you expect to see from a Trump Presidency? **Restoration of the Constitution, rule of law, and common sense.**

9. How would a President Trump help your family? **Make me proud to be an American.**

10. Do you think Mr. Trump is straightforward with his plans for the country? **Somewhat. But I agree that you shouldn't show all your card.**

11. In your opinion, would a President Trump secure our borders and protect the United States from terrorist? **YES**

12. Are family and/or friends treating you differently because of your support for Mr. Trump? **NO**

13. Have you been to a Trump Rally? And if so, would you tell about your experience. **NO**

14. Do you trust Donald J. Trump? **YES!**

15. How will you feel on election day if Donald Trump becomes our President Elect? **Ecstatic**

16. How will you feel on election day if Donald Trump loses?
Depressed

Additional Comments:

He's the right man for our time. I believe God has raised him up, prepared him to lead our country out of the darkness we find ourselves in.

ANONYMOUS VOTER

Date: **1/8/2016**
Age: **60, Male**
Level of Education: **High School**
Lives in **Chattanooga, TN.**
Party Affiliation: **Independent**
In 2012 our anonymous voter **wrote in the name of Rand Paul for President.**

1. What is the first word that comes to mind when you hear the name Donald J. Trump? **TUFF**

2. What do you consider Trump's strongest personal trait? **TRUTH**

3. What do you consider Trump's weakest personal trait? **ARROGANT**

4. How do you feel about Mr. Trump's family values? **VERY GOOD**

5. Are you concerned with his past marriages and bankruptcies? **NO**

6. Does it concern you that Mr. Trump was a Democrat before he was a Republican and has donated to both sides? **NO**

7. What concerns you most about the path our country is currently on? **Generally all roads we are taking lead straight to hell.**

8. What do you expect to see from a Trump Presidency? **The beginning of a turn around.**

9. How would a President Trump help your family? **Give us hope!**

10. Do you think Mr. Trump is straightforward with his plans for the country? **Yes, Yes, Yes**

11. In your opinion, would a President Trump secure our borders and protect the United States from terrorist? **Yes**

12. Are family and/or friends treating you differently because of your support for Mr. Trump? **Yes**

13. Have you been to a Trump Rally? And if so, would you tell about your experience. **Yes, the atmosphere was electric.**

14. Do you trust Donald J. Trump? **Yes**

15. How will you feel on election day if Donald Trump becomes our President Elect? **Happy and relieved**

16. How will you feel on election day if Donald Trump loses?
Looking at moving to Central America!!!!!!

KAREN D.

Date: **1/8/2016**
Age: **59, Female**
Level of Education: **LPN**
Lives in **Warsaw, MO**
Party Affiliation: **Republican**
In 2012 Karen **voted for Mitt Romney**

1. What is the first word that comes to mind when you hear the name Donald J. Trump? **God-sent**

2. What do you consider Trumps strongest personal trait? **HONESTY**

3. What do you consider Trumps weakest personal trait? **Naive to press lies (no more!)**

4. How do you feel about Mr. Trump's family values? **Love it. He is a real American. Rich, but real.**

5. Are you concerned with his past marriages and bankruptcies? **No. I am no saint.**

6. Does it concern you that Mr. Trump was a Democrat before he was a Republican and has donated to both sides? **No. I am in business 40 years and know how it WORKS.**

7. What concerns you most about the path our country is currently on? **National Security**

8. What do you expect to see from a Trump Presidency? **Safety, JOBS, economic health.**

9. How would a President Trump help your family? **Protect us from Illegals/Muslims.**

10. Do you think Mr. Trump is straightforward with his plans for the country? **YES.**

11. In your opinion, would a President Trump secure our borders and protect the United States from terrorist? **YES.**

12. Are family and/or friends treating you differently because of your support for Mr. Trump? **NO. ALL FOR TRUMP.**

13. Have you been to a Trump Rally? And if so, would you tell about your experience. **No but will when he comes near MO.**

14. Do you trust Donald J. Trump? **YES**

15. How will you feel on election day if Donald Trump becomes our President Elect? **I will celebrate for 3 days !!!**

16. How will you feel on election day if Donald Trump loses? **Ohhhhh I don't want to THINK about it. Personally, I would leave the country if there were a place to go. Depression at the thought of him losing or murdered by the bass-turds in DC.**

Additional Comments:
MAKE AMERICA GREAT AGAIN !!!!! PRAY TRUMP CAN be God's vessel for turning this country back to HIM. PS I am an Evangelical Christian .

DEBORAH

Date: **1/17/2016**
Age: **63, Female**
Level of Education: **High School**
Lives in **Plainfield, Illinois**
Party Affiliation: **Republican**
In 2012, Deborah **declined to vote.**

1. What is the first word that comes to mind when you hear the name Donald J. Trump? **Strong**

2. What do you consider Trump's strongest personal trait? **Knowledge**

3. What do you consider Trump's weakest personal trait? N**one**

4. How do you feel about Mr. Trump's family values? **Great family!**

5. Are you concerned with his past marriages and bankruptcies? **NO!**

6. Does it concern you that Mr. Trump was a Democrat before he was a Republican and has donated to both sides? **NO!**

7. What concerns you most about the path our country is currently on? **Corruption in govt.**

8. What do you expect to see from a Trump Presidency? T**he opposite of now.**

9. How would a President Trump help your family?
By insuring our National security, financial security, America working again.

10. Do you think Mr. Trump is straightforward with his plans for the country? **Definitely**

11. In your opinion, would a President Trump secure our borders and protect the United States from terrorist? **Yes**

12. Are family and/or friends treating you differently because of your support for Mr. Trump? **NO**

13. Have you been to a Trump Rally? And if so, would you tell about your experience. **NO**

14. Do you trust Donald J. Trump? **100%**

15. How will you feel on election day if Donald Trump becomes our President Elect? **SAFE**

16. How will you feel on election day if Donald Trump loses? **SCARED**

Additional Comments:
Mr. Trump is his own man, he continues to educate those who are unaware of the current dissent of USA. I thank God daily for Donald Trump. I am a huge twitter supporter among many who want ONLY TRUMP.

WENDY D.

Date: **1/18/16**
Age: **50, Female**
Level of Education: **Bachelor of Arts**
Lives in **Glasgow, Missouri**
Party Affiliation: **Republican**
In 2012, she **voted for Mitt Romney.**

1. What is the first word that comes to mind when you hear the name Donald J. Trump? **Fearless**

2. What do you consider Trump's strongest personal trait? **Straight shooter....tells the truth.**

3. What do you consider Trump's weakest personal trait? **NONE**

4. How do you feel about Mr. Trump's family values? **I love everything about this man and how he has kept his children involved in his empire and his daily life.**

5. Are you concerned with his past marriages and bankruptcies? **No...it proves he is a doer. Everyone falls down BUT only the ambitious and strong get back up and try again.**

6. Does it concern you that Mr. Trump was a Democrat before he was a Republican and has donated to both sides? **NO....I was a Republican for 32 years BUT I would vote for Mr. Trump if he had to stand as an independent. I believe BOTH the GOP and**

the Democrats are so corrupt they don't know how
to be honorable anymore.

7. What concerns you most about the path our
country is currently on? **MUSLIMS! They are
disgusting. After them, all illegals.**

8. What do you expect to see from a Trump
Presidency?
**Closed borders, expelled Muslims and a
stronger freer America!**

9. How would a President Trump help your family?
**I believe that if we don't expel Muslims and illegals,
my children have no future in America. WE ARE
WILLING TO LEAVE! My oldest son is already
an Ex-Patriot!**

10. Do you think Mr. Trump is straightforward
with his plans for the country? **YES!**

11. In your opinion, would a President Trump
secure our borders and protect the United States from
terrorist? **YES!**

12. Are family and/or friends treating you
differently because of your support for Mr. Trump?
**YES....the family has turned their back on my
children and me because we aren't stupid liberals.**

13. Have you been to a Trump Rally? And if so,
would you tell about your experience. **No....but how I
would LOVE to.**

14. Do you trust Donald J. Trump? **YES, YES, YES**

15. How will you feel on election day if Donald Trump becomes our President Elect? **Like there might be hope for America to rise from the hell-hole Obama and the democrats have put us in.**

16. How will you feel on election day if Donald Trump loses? **We will probably leave America and move to the Far East. I have no desire to live in a Muslim hell-hole.**

Additional Comments:
Trump 2016!

ALLY L.

Date: **1/17/2016**
Age: **32, Female**
Level of Education: **Post graduate study**
Lives in **West Hartford, CT**
Party Affiliation: **Republican**
In 2012, she **voted for Mitt Romney.**

1. What is the first word that comes to mind when you hear the name Donald J. Trump? **Brilliant**

2. What do you consider Trump's strongest personal trait? **His love for America!**

3. What do you consider Trump's weakest personal trait? **None**

4. How do you feel about Mr. Trump's family values? **Great!!! I love his family values.**

5. Are you concerned with his past marriages and bankruptcies? **No**

6. Does it concern you that Mr. Trump was a Democrat before he was a Republican and has donated to both sides? **No people change parties and views all the time.**

7. What concerns you most about the path our country is currently on? **It's going to hell.**

8. What do you expect to see from a Trump Presidency? **I expect that America will thrive and become great again.**

9. How would a President Trump help your family? **Put more money in our pockets.**

10. Do you think Mr. Trump is straightforward with his plans for the country? **Yes very straightforward.**

11. In your opinion, would a President Trump secure our borders and protect the United States from terrorist? **Oh absolutely!! He will build that wall!!**

12. Are family and/or friends treating you differently because of your support for Mr. Trump? **No**

13. Have you been to a Trump Rally? And if so, would you tell about your experience. **No but would love to attend one.**

14. Do you trust Donald J. Trump? **Totally!!!**

15. How will you feel on election day if Donald Trump becomes our President Elect? **I will be happy for the first time in almost 8 years.**

16. How will you feel on election day if Donald Trump loses? **I will be angry!!!!!**

Additional Comments:

I LOVE DONALD TRUMP!!!!

MICHAEL W.

Date: **1/14/2016**
Age: **39, Male**
Level of Education: **College Graduate**
Lives in **Scottsville, KY**
Party Affiliation: **Republican**
In 2012 Michael **voted for Mitt Romney.**

1. What is the first word that comes to mind when you hear the name Donald J. Trump? **Leader**

2. What do you consider Trump's strongest personal trait? **Confidence**

3. What do you consider Trump's weakest personal trait? **N/A**

4. How do you feel about Mr. Trump's family values? **He has a wonderful family who loves this country.**

5. Are you concerned with his past marriages and bankruptcies? **I have been married twice before so no.**

6. Does it concern you that Mr. Trump was a Democrat before he was a Republican and has donated to both sides? **As was Ronald Reagan.**

7. What concerns you most about the path our country is currently on? **Socialism**

8. What do you expect to see from a Trump Presidency? **A border wall with a strong economy. If Donald Trump can fix immigration and trade the rest of the issues will take care of themselves.**

9. How would a President Trump help your family? **I'm more concerned with Donald Trump helping this country. If he does that our family will benefit.**

10. Do you think Mr. Trump is straightforward with his plans for the country? **Absolutely, read his plans on his website and you will understand.**

11. In your opinion, would a President Trump secure our borders and protect the United States from terrorist? **Without a doubt.**

12. Are family and/or friends treating you differently because of your support for Mr. Trump? **All of my family supports Mr. Trump.**

13. Have you been to a Trump Rally? And if so, would you tell about your experience. **I would go to show my support however my mind is made up.**

14. Do you trust Donald J. Trump? **Yes**

15. How will you feel on election day if Donald Trump becomes our President Elect? **As if the country has been saved and that God has not turned his back on America.**

16. How will you feel on election day if Donald Trump loses? **Disappointed**

Additional Comments:
Trump 2016!

VICKI C.

Date: **1/8/2016**
Age: **60, Female**
Level of Education: **Some College**
Lives in **Garner, NC**
Party Affiliation: **Republican**
In 2012, she **chose not** to vote.

1. What is the first word that comes to mind when you hear the name Donald J. Trump? **Defend**

2. What do you consider Trump's strongest personal trait? **Attribute is his leadership skills in very complicated matters.**

3. What do you consider Trump's weakest personal trait? **The Donald has no weaknesses.**

4. How do you feel about Mr. Trump's family values? **People talk about Mr. Trump's tone as though it's a bad thing. I admire his ability to speak his mind and not hold back.**

5. Are you concerned with his past marriages and bankruptcies? **I'm voting for a person who has the intelligence and proven ability to get the job done. Trump is the only one who can clean up the mess this Country is in. I'm divorced myself so don't care about his past marriages.**

6. Does it concern you that Mr. Trump was a Democrat before he was a Republican and has donated

to both sides? **It concerns me that the establishment is so against Trump, but if that is how they want to play then we will vote them all out!**

7. What concerns you most about the path our country is currently on? **I am concerned that lots of cheating will occur in this election because I've always been skeptical about those extra votes in Florida Jeb found for his brother!**

8. What do you expect to see from a Trump Presidency? **I expect a President to show strong leadership skills and to do what the citizens of this Country want done.**

9. How would a President Trump help your family? **President Trump will unite our Country and make us safe, powerful and loved.**

10. Do you think Mr. Trump is straightforward with his plans for the country? **I think Donald is a genius.**

11. In your opinion, would a President Trump secure our borders and protect the United States from terrorist?
A President Trump will be the best thing this Country has had since Washington!

12. Are family and/or friends treating you differently because of your support for Mr. Trump?
For the most part my family is for Trump, but I see a big difference in the younger and older

generations. **The younger see the world and accept it, the older want things the way it used to be before terrorism.**

13. Have you been to a Trump Rally? And if so, would you tell about your experience. **One of the highlights of my life was seeing Trump in person and it's the only time in my life I've ever even wanted to see a politician! It just somehow made me feel safer in his presence.**

14. Do you trust Donald J. Trump? **I've watched Trump over the years and have always been an admirer. I trust him because he always tells the truth and loves the USA and the American people.**

15. How will you feel on election day if Donald Trump becomes our President Elect? **Exhilarated!**

16. How will you feel on election day if Donald Trump loses? **Not gonna happen!!!**

Additional Comments:
Donald Trump is the Real Deal! A true patriot who is the only candidate offering his talents to us for no other reason than because he loves the USA!

BARB A.

Date: **1/15/2016**
Age: **Female, no age reference**
Level of Education: **Master's Degree**
Lives in **Cincinnati, Ohio**
Party Affiliation: **Independent**
In 2012, she **voted for Mitt Romney.**

1. What is the first word that comes to mind when you hear the name Donald J. Trump? **Sincere**

2. What do you consider Trump's strongest personal trait? **Honest**

3. What do you consider Trump's weakest personal trait? **Bragging**

4. How do you feel about Mr. Trump's family values? **To be admired.**

5. Are you concerned with his past marriages and bankruptcies? **Not the least! I do not give one sheet!**

6. Does it concern you that Mr. Trump was a Democrat before he was a Republican and has donated to both sides? **Not at all. So what.**

7. What concerns you most about the path our country is currently on? **Political corruption.**

8. What do you expect to see from a Trump Presidency? **Strength, Respect**

9. How would a President Trump help your family? **Restore faith in this country.**

10. Do you think Mr. Trump is straightforward with his plans for the country? **Yes!**

11. In your opinion, would a President Trump secure our borders and protect the United States from terrorist? **Absolutely**

12. Are family and/or friends treating you differently because of your support for Mr. Trump? **No, they all support Trump.**

13. Have you been to a Trump Rally? And if so, would you tell about your experience. **N/A**

14. Do you trust Donald J. Trump? **100%**

15. How will you feel on election day if Donald Trump becomes our President Elect? **Elated**

16. How will you feel on election day if Donald Trump loses? **Depressed, Cheated**

Additional Comments:
The RNC/DNC will not stop the PEOPLE'S vote this time!

THE MILLENNIALS OF OUR NATION

The Millennial played a huge role in the election of Barack Obama in 2008 and again in 2012 but who exactly are these people?

Millennial's are a difficult demographic to pin down. There are no precise dates when the generation starts and stops but most assume that a millennial is someone who was born somewhere between the early 1980's and the early 2000's.

There are approximately some 81 million children who fall within this category and will be the generation to replace the Baby-Boomers as they retire.

The millennial's have different characteristics than previous generations as they've grown up in a world quite different than the one we all knew.

They've been plugged into technology since the day they were born, growing up needing the instant gratification that goes with the frantic pace of the Internet.

They are the "safe generation", living in environments that are almost completely harmless and germ free. The children of this generation don't go outside much because there is just no need to. They have everything they want in the palm of their hands, literally.

They were never allowed to fail at anything they ever did and if they did fail, they got rewarded with a pat on the back from mommy saying "That was great, Little Bobby (or Little Susie). So what if you struck-out eighteen times, you are still a winner." Then off they will run to get their "participation" trophy.

Millennials don't believe in the value of face-to-face contact but this is not to say that they aren't social creatures. They build amazing networks of their peers on-line and use these as their sole means of communication but living life outside that world oftentimes makes it difficult if not impossible for some to succeed later in life.

Face time, to millennials I know first-hand, is more valuable when there's less of it, or reserved for only really important talks, and they especially want it to be a quick hit-and-run.

I've raised four millennials and I can attest to these truths. They want what they want, when they want it and they don't care what they have to do to get it.

This is, of course, a direct consequence of technology, as the availability of the world makes instant gratification possible in the first place. But it's more than that.

This generation has been said to be lazy, when in actuality they get a lot done. They are tremendous multi-taskers as they seem to have been born with technology in their blood as many can learn the intricacies of a complicated cell phone long before they learn to speak.

What I see is a generation that believes in the efficiency of technology as a means for maximum output.

They recognize that the only way to have it all is to work at maximum efficiency when they do work. For the millennial entrepreneur that means few, if any, face-to-face meetings with more conference calls, video messaging, emails and text. It means results without getting bogged down in the human side of life.

They will be the first generation for which Hispanics and Latinos will be the largest minority group in the country instead of African Americans. And I am proud to say that studies show that millennials have the most educated mothers of any generation before them.[135]

Millennials are likely to be more educated then other generations but they aren't as likely to find jobs in their field of study as the job markets become scarcer for them every day.

They are the most scheduled generation ever, and as true multi-taskers, they expect to have many different careers in their lifetime.

They are a diverse generation and generally have an easier time of accepting the "out of the norm" attitudes which thrive in today's alternative society. In their somewhat sheltered opinion, the more diverse their environment is, the happier they think they will be.

The political attitudes among Millennials in the United States tend to be more supportive of social liberal policies and same-sex marriage relative to other demographics, though less supportive of abortion than earlier generations. They are also more likely to oppose things such as animal testing for medical purposes while they believe in global warming and are typically environmentally conscious.

Millennials tend to be social liberals and fiscal centrists, that is until they are forced to actually enter the real world. Once they get jobs and begin to pay income taxes they become more aware and lean towards conservatism on fiscal issues while remaining liberal on the social side.

What are millennial's looking for in a candidate this year.

In 2008, the millennial vote went overwhelmingly for the young, charismatic Barack Obama. He promised them "Hope and Change" at a time when they were craving exactly that. They may not have listened to the words of Barack Obama but they were definitely drawn to his youth, charms and good looks.

They steadfastly gave him their trust and their vote, and hoped for the best. Unfortunately, they didn't get what they were looking for from President Obama.

He let them down by his utter disinterest in creating jobs for them. They'd worked hard in college, most of them amassing huge college loan debt with the assumption that a job would be waiting for them in the end. But the job market is now ruthless with the majority of the competition for these new graduates being the illegal immigrants that the Obama Administration has flooded into the country.

Jobs are few and wages are deflated as the job market becomes saturated with applicants, qualified and not.

Employers are given incentives by the Obama Administration for hiring immigrants, legal or otherwise, over our own American children. It has even gotten so desperate that unemployed adults have been forced to take low-end jobs in fast food or retail in order to support themselves and their families, further reducing the available options for the young.

My own children know this first hand. I have three daughters and a son, two of my girls have recently graduated college and the other one will graduate next year. They've all taken out student loans and have worked really hard. I couldn't be prouder of them all. But at the same time, I am sad for them, too.

Karen, my oldest, is married to a college graduate. He's a good man, clean cut and he graduated with very high marks. His name is Nathan and he expected, like so many other college graduates, that he'd find a job relatively quickly. That was six years ago.

Nathan has sent out hundreds of resumes to companies all over the country but until just recently, he never received any call-backs. He was becoming discouraged, feeling like all the time and money he'd spent on college was wasted and being forced to work at a Lowes when he had a degree in Accounting was hard for him to swallow.

We all watched as Nathan became more and more despondent trying desperately to provide for my daughter and grandson. It broke my heart to watch this self-confident young man being torn down by the collapse of our economy and the negligence of a president to do anything about it. The future seemed hopeless to my son-in-law when out of the blue, he received a phone call. It was from a company in the same small town they lived in and it was the first company Nathan had applied to six years ago.

He went in for the interview and he nailed it. They hired him straight-away and three months later, he got a small promotion.

Today Nathan is only days away from finishing Grad School and he is taking such remarkable care of his small family, my daughter and grandson and I couldn't be any prouder of him. It took him six years and loads of self-doubt but he is one of the lucky ones.

He finally has his shot at the American Dream. Isn't that all anybody wants?

Where do Millennials stand on Donald Trump?

Millennials are the most studied voting bloc in the country, not only because they are plentiful but because they are also the most diverse and impressionable.

The Democrat Party has held reign over this particular voting bloc ever since they were old enough to vote which has ensured the Democrats a path to the White House and Congressional control for many years.

But, as I stated earlier, once the millennial graduated to the ranks of a tax-paying citizen, their young idealistic attitudes began to slowly disappear.

For the first time, things became hard for them. Their parents were no longer able to provide them with the moon and the stars, and they began to see just how hard real life really was.

These past eight years have been a real eye-opener for the Millennial as they've been forced to learn what failure means. They've fought their way through the poor economy, throughout the past eight years, doing everything they can to survive. With high unemployment, massive student loan debt, the ever-looming nightmare of Obamacare, and the soaring costs of living, they feel as if the American Dream is no longer available to them.

The top issue for millennials revolve around the economy with the most important issues being, in order of relevance, jobs, national debt, unemployment, taxes, government spending, and financial stability.

Millennials tend to carry a positive view of capitalism and most believe that corporations who earn profits are entitled to keep them. According to the Reason-Rupp latest polling data 52 percent of millennials favor capitalism over socialism and 64 percent favor the free market over a government managed economy.[136]

Donald Trump represents the kind of success that can be attained though capitalism and the free market, two things that the Democrats attempt to villainize but that are actually considered a positive for millennials.

Most millennials also don't believe that corporate profits are too high or that corporate taxes are too low, which goes to show an evolving generation that is beginning to realize that the success of American corporations means better and higher paying jobs for them.

Today's millennial also understands that when the government intervenes with costly regulations and over taxation, jobs and profits are driven overseas which in turn leaves them unemployed. Could it be that they've finally seen the light?

Donald Trump represents the American Dream to today's millennial, a dream that is only attained through hard work and a free market economy. A commanding 64 percent of millennial's say hard work is the key to success and 40 percent say that poor choices and lack of work ethic is what causes poverty in this country. They've come to realize that we all start at the same place and what we do with our lives, is really up to each of us. This is the exact opposite view held by most Democrats in office today.

All of these changes in the long-held attitudes of the millennial towards wealth, poverty, taxation, and the free market economy can only strengthen the presidential candidacy of Donald Trump.

Just as they failed to listen to the words of a young, charismatic junior Senator from Chicago, biting them in the butt, they are listening to every word Donald Trump has to say and they like what they hear.

In Donald Trump, the millennials of this country see a man who will be able to bring America's economy back to its former glory. They see his track record a job creation and they know he is a skilled negotiator who will fight for their futures, like President Obama promised to do, but failed.

These changes of ideology in many of the views held by millennials has created a huge opening, not only for Donald Trump, but for any candidates who believes that a free market economy with less intrusive regulations and lower taxation is the key to Making America Great Again.

THE VOICE OF THE PEOPLE

Avatar: Vulgarian:
THE MOTHER OF CONSERVATISM:
"If anyone needed more evidence of why the American people are suffering at the hands of their own government, look no further than the budget deal announced by Speaker Ryan. In order to avoid a government shutdown, a cowardly threat from an incompetent President, the elected Republicans in Congress threw in the towel and showed absolutely no budget discipline.

The American people will have to absorb higher deficits, greater debt, less economic liberty and more corporate welfare. Congress cannot seem to help itself in bending to every whim of special interests. How can they face their constituents when they continue to burden our children and grandchildren with debts they will never be able to repay? Our government is failing us, so we must do something about it. Who knows how bad things will be when the next administration comes in and has to pick up the pieces?

The only special interest not being served by our government is the American people. It is time we imposed budget discipline by holding the line on spending, getting rid of waste, fraud and abuse, and by taking on our debt. To do these things, we need a President who can lead the fight to hold Congress and the rest of government accountable. Together, we will Make America Great Again."

Avatar: ronnieD:

"TO THE MEDIA and any other brain dead hack out there. I intend to vote for Trump. I honestly have little or no clue about his personal life and times other than what any person has seen in the news over the years. Discounting at least 50% of your so called news about the guy as being spin. I would say he is a good and honorable man. He is certainly a highly talented well educated businessman. He clearly has a lot of want-to-be players who envy him, his family, his money.

I also find that I spend zero time thinking about his wealth at all in any way at all for any reason at all.

I do enjoy seeing him open up his world to the kids – a tour of his jet, his helicopter, his helicopter rides for the kids. Very cool man!!

I find I support Trump because he has the will and the ability to man up and tell it to us like it is. The illegals for example coming out of Mexico daily for countless years and the harm it has caused Americans in America but one of many examples. And of course nowadays it is illegal Mexicans and outright terrorists crossing into the USA.

I also realize Trump doesn't know it all, no problem, neither do you, neither do I. I also realize once in office as president of the USA Trump will find his way through the maze of Democrats and Republicans who are outright hacks and deal with it.

Trump will do what he says he will do.

I dare say Trump will get to the heart of things RAPIDLY.

Much faster than you (media) or any other GOP candidate can and would!!

And I do expect him to, in some way or other, start to fire people and replace them with true talent. As a taxpayer I DESERVE his efforts.

That is where I am coming from. You really are trash these days (media). Just a bunch of low flying low life liars and spinners to the max.

I have YOUR number. I am not YOUR friend. you may depend on that much here and now."

Avatar: drattastic:
"Like it or not we are the new Republican Party and we are Nationalist.

We want illegals gone.
We want our borders secured.
We want no new Muslims because they don't play well with others.
We want Americans to be taken care of first .
We want America first .
We want our Vets put on a pedestal.
We don't care if you're Black as long as you love America.
We don't care if you're Hispanic as long as you're legal.
We don't care if your Gay, that's between you and God.
We don't care if you're pro-choice, that's between you and God.
We're cool with Christianity but don't think it's everything.
We don't like globalist and greedy corporate a-holes.

We like our guns and if you don't, just don't F**K with ours.

We HATE Political Correctness.

We don't want Obamacare or single payer but we think the poor should   be taken care of .

We like Social Security because we F**King paid for it .

We want a strong military and if we have to use them we won't tie their hands behind their backs.

We're tired of the lying politicians in both parties and we are going to put a stop to the BS.

You can take your globalist BS and shove it up your bought and paid for asses Hillary, Robotio, Jeb!, Kasich and yes, Goldman Sachs Ted.

Trump 2016!"

Avatar: Preacher: shares his wish list for a Trump Administration. These are right in line with everything else I'm hearing from Americans who took the time to answer my on-line survey. They are:

MY LIST:

1. Build the Wall and Secure our freaking borders.
2. Bring down our national debt
3. Rebuild the Military that BO has destroyed.
4. Get the economy roaring.
5. Scrap Obamacare and Common Core.
6. Leave my guns alone and leave the 2nd Amendment alone.
7. Jobs, jobs and more jobs. We need jobs.

I don't care if Trump gave money to Hillary, Harry Reid, Pelosi or whoever. He didn't give them money to help them, he gave to help himself and his business. Purely selfish reasons. He buys politicians. That is good business. Now I would take issue with his donations if I thought he wanted to help people like Pelosi and Hillary.

I don't care if Trump is not very Conservative. I don't need him to be conservative, just fix the things on my list. Big money is not going to own him.

I don't care if Trump is not a good Christian. I'm not saying he is not, I wouldn't make that judgment. But he understands that Christians and Jews are under siege and he plans to put a stop to it. His relationship with God is between him and Him.

I don't care if Trump has New York Values. I don't even know what that means. Just fix the stuff on my list.

I don't care if Trump is rude, crude and socially unacceptable. Just fix the stuff on my list.

I don't care if you call me or Trump a racist, nativist, xenophobe, homophobic, or jerk. Just fix the stuff on my list.

I don't care if Trump is in favor of eminent domain. He believes the land owners should be well compensated. You can't build the Keystone Pipeline without it. But it is not something a president would use. Just fix the stuff on my list."

Avatar: Glenn: "History will prove Trump to be the George Washington of our time!"

Avatar: Pete Peterson:
"I haven't been a Trump guy but this is the reason people like me are leaning towards Trump. We feel let down by our party and what it stands for, Trump is shaking things up and the establishment Republicans

don't like it because it will affect their gravy train, which makes them no different from Democrats."

Avatar: zanzamander:
"Essentially the GOP is dead. And if they don't win against Hillary, then they'll be buried as well.

I don't count Trump as a Republican, I honestly think he is a swing voter himself. He stands for USA and is seeing the whole country going to pot and there is no one at the helm to rescue it. He is an Independent.

So apart from Cruz, who himself is loathed by his own party, can you name any GOP politicians who are any different to the Democrats?

In UK we have a choice between an extreme left party (Labour) and a Socialist one (Tory). There is no traditional main stream right wing national party - well Ukip, I guess but they have a mountain to climb."

Avatar: Mark E:
"TRUMP is not supposed to try to win. He's expected to be attacked by the establishment and then pack it in. People see it all too clearly, that's why he's getting so much support. People can see how TRUMP is winning everything and they want this man as their POTUS."

Avatar: jhpeters:
"I was very impressed, when at the debate, Trump said he was going to concentrate on the state of the nation and let his wife and kids run the corporation. Getting America better will be his focus. He is the only truly altruistic candidate that I can see. I agree that we

can see what's going on with the RNC and the Bush clan, being to keep all the has-beens in the race to dilute the percentage of the primary vote and deny Trump 51% going into the convention."

Avatar: patriotrenegade:
"The CFR, Trilaterals, Bilderbergs, CFR owned media, and the banksters have always put shills into the race. We've had 11 straight elections of CFR v CFR with 20 years of Bush/Clintoons. In 2012 the shills were McCain, Huntsman, Perry, and Gingrich. This time it's Jeb, Carly, Rubio, Cruz, and Perry again (out). NO MORE OF THIS. Trump is the only real American left. GO TRUMP!"

Avatar: Terry Jenkins:
"We will win. Southerners love Trump, Northerners love Trump, Americans love Trump, Patriots love Trump and Law Enforcement Love Trump. Iran is scared of Trump just like they were of President Reagan. Mr. Trump Make America Great Again. We got your back."

Avatar: Tony Arroyo:
"Tony Arroyo Dear Mr. Future President can you tell me what really happened in Benghazi? I watched that film yesterday and it truly made me mad. I started chanting your name for President when the film was over wished I filmed it . I Know you would never leave our people to Die . "Trump for President".

Avatar: John Kurkosky:

"Donald J. Trump, instilling trust that together we can make America Greater than ever before, securing Americas future keeping our country safe and restoring faith, hope and pride that our greatest days are ahead, this movement is spreading across our lands and will be historic."

Avatar: Roger Dean:
This country is finished if we don't vote for Donald J Trump! Ted Cruz (Grandpa Munster) could never win in a general election. Trump 2016!

Avatar: Kathryn A. Burkett:
"I'm just praying that all the people who want Mr. Trump will actually vote for him. Remember there will be voter fraud going on just like in the last two elections, so we have to be out in a large number to get him in."

Avatar: Paul Lorang:
"I take that responsibility very serious and would never consider not voting...Go Donald Trump 2016, Make America Great Again....You have my vote!"

Avatar: James Snotherly:
"Some folks call "The Donald" a buffoon. But how smart can he be to turn a $million into over $8 billion. And, I would say that Donald gives a lot of his money to charity. I think Donald is pretty intelligent beyond most people's imagination; I think he is a great role model. He tells it like it is. I know many "Christians" who don't live the clean life Trump does. What impressed me with his 20/20 interview, he said he

doesn't like to embarrass anyone. That is exactly what my Mother told me 70 years ago. "Never embarrass anyone in public."

"As it is now, I will vote for Trump."

Avatar: V.I.P.:

"I admit I originally was skeptical of Trump but he eventually won me over by doing everything the establishment says you shouldn't do. He uses clear and straight talk with no double meanings or ambiguities. No watered down bureaucratic political correctness. Trump has changed the game when it comes to American politics forever. I am convinced more than ever that he's the real deal!"

Avatar: Rainbowrider:

"As a skilled blue collar worker Donald Trump is my middle finger to the establishment status quo."

Avatar: Affercat:

"Trump supporters are already a 3rd party. We do not support the Democrat leanings of the current GOPe. After the 2012 final betrayal, the old RINO party is dead. The new party will be called the Republican Party."

Avatar: Sam Waters:

"That's correct. The party is changing the guardians. The current leadership of the party no longer reflects the base. Many of the media members who are partisans are having trouble adjusting."

Avatar: IWantThe50sBack:

"WE ARE EXACTLY 1 YEAR- 365 DAYS, FROM PRESIDENT TRUMP'S INAUGURATION!!! TRUMP 2016 AND 2020!!!"

Avatar: bonni:
"God help us survive and bring this forth. So we can once again be One Nation Under God Indivisible with Liberty and Justice for All."

COUNTDOWN TO IOWA

NO WORRIES

Donald Trump jumped into the 2016 presidential race to the surprise of many, and has since taken the lead in the national polls.

Trump's plain-spoken campaigning has raised the ire of those in the mainstream media, but his decidedly un-politically correct speech has won him huge swaths of supporters across the country.

Gathered below are 15 of Trump's quotes that have impacted the 2016 election cycle, according to Newsmax.com. [137]

1. "We need somebody who can take the brand of the United States and make it great again. Ladies and gentlemen: I am officially running for president of the United States, and we are going to make our country great again." Campaign kickoff (June 2015) [138]

2. "When Mexico sends its people, they're not sending their best. . . they're sending people that have lots of problems . . . they're bringing drugs, they're bringing crime. They're rapists. And some, I assume, are good people." Campaign kickoff (June 2015) [139]

3. "I would build a great wall, and nobody builds walls better than me. Believe me. And I'll build it very inexpensively. I'll build a great, great wall on our southern border and I will have Mexico pay for that wall. Mark my words." Campaign kickoff (June 2015)[140]

4. "You have to bring in jobs, you have to take the jobs back from China, you have to take the jobs back from Mexico." CNN interview (June 2015)[141]

5. "New Hampshire has a tremendous drug epidemic. I am going to create borders. No drugs are coming in. We're going to build a wall . . . They will stop coming to New Hampshire. They will stop coming to our country."
Republican debate (Feb. 2016)[142]

6. "Never, ever, ever in my life have I seen any transaction so incompetently negotiated as our deal with Iran. And I mean never . . . Israel will not survive."
Political rally (Sept. 2015)[143]

7. "Donald J. Trump is calling for a total and complete shutdown of Muslims entering the United States until our country's representatives can figure out what is going on." Campaign rally (Dec. 2015)[144]

8. "They have sections in Paris that are radicalized, where the police refuse to go there. They're petrified. The police refuse to go in there."
MSNBC interview (Dec. 2015)[145]

9. "When you get these terrorists, you have to take out their families . . . When they say they don't care about their lives, you have to take out their families."
— Fox News interview (Dec. 2015)[146]

10. "I watched when the World Trade Center came tumbling down. And I watched in Jersey City, New Jersey, where thousands and thousands of people were cheering as that building was coming down.
Thousands of people were cheering." Campaign rally (Nov. 2015)[147]

11. "I would bring back water-boarding, and I would bring back a hell of a lot worse than water-boarding. You can rest assured that as commander in chief, I would use whatever enhanced interrogation methods we could to keep this country safe."
Republican primary debate (Feb. 2016)[148]

12. "It's in the book that he's got a pathological temper. That's a big problem because you don't cure that." on Ben Carson's troubled childhood (Nov. 2015)[149]

13. "I supported him for president, I raised a million dollars for him, that's a lot of money, I supported him, he lost, he let us down. But you know, he lost, so I've never liked him as much after that, because I don't like losers . . . He's not a war hero . . . He's a war hero because he was captured. I like people that weren't captured." on Sen. John McCain, Family Leadership Summit (July 2015)[150]

14. "I've gone to gay weddings. I've been at gay weddings. I have been against [same-sex marriage] from the standpoint of the Bible, from the standpoint of my teachings as growing up and going to Sunday school and going to church." Bloomberg interview (Aug. 2015)[151]

15. "Everybody's got to be covered. This is an un-Republican thing for me to say . . . I am going to take care of everybody. I don't care if it costs me votes or not. Everybody's going to be taken care of much better than they're taken care of now."
— on his health care plan, "60 Minutes" interview (Sept. 2015)[152]

It doesn't seem to matter what Donald Trump says and when the media dares to criticize him, he only gets more popular. For Trump supporters, there seems to be nothing their candidate can do to lose them.

The media has proclaimed his campaign dead with each controversial comment, but they fail to realize, the American People don't care what he does, as long as he continues to shake up the process.

DITCHING THE DEBATE

Tonight is the sixth Republican debate, hosted by Fox News. The moderators are Bret Baier, Chris Wallace and none other than, Megyn Kelly herself. The first 2016 Republican Debate in Cleveland Ohio, was moderated by these same three and as the 24 million of us who watched it know, there was quite a bit of controversy with that one.

Donald Trump and Megyn Kelly became immersed in a war of words over what many thought were sexist and inappropriate questions asked by Ms. Kelly.

Megyn began her questioning of Mr. Trump with a speech stating that in the past he'd made disparaging and often-times sexist remarks about women. She went on about comments he had made toward women, calling them "fat pigs," "dogs," "slobs" and "disgusting animals." (which were all true enough in the case of Rosie O'Donnell) then ended by declaring, not asking, but declaring that Donald Trump was part of the so-called "War On Women" and how was he going to beat Hillary Clinton given that he is part of the problem?

This was all nonsense on Ms. Kelly's part, a stunt orchestrated to make women hate Donald Trump.

Ms. Kelly was allegedly overheard before the debate saying that (paraphrasing) 'Before the night was over, there would be one less candidate in the race.' She was talking about Donald Trump. Ms. Kelly made it her personal mission to destroy our candidate that night but she failed miserably.

Donald Trump has said the things she described but only in response to things being said to him. Such is the case with Rosie O'Donnell. Trump is a counter-puncher, he fights back but he doesn't usually start the fight.

In no way is Trump anti-woman. A lot of the highest positions within the Trump organization are held by women. His own daughter, Ivanka is one of the strongest women I've ever seen and if she'd been raised by a father who had anything less than the utmost respect for women, then Ivanka Trump would not be the capable and successful business woman, wife and mother she is today.

It was her father's love, support and respect that enabled her to feel secure enough to put herself out there in the first place.

It was her father, Donald Trump, who instilled in her the knowledge that she is capable of achieving anything she wants to be, with hard work and determination.

After raising three daughters myself, one a liberal, I can tell you that if he'd shown any disrespect for women whatsoever, he would not be married to one of the most beautiful women in the world today, while raising confident and caring women in Ivanka and Tiffany.

Jimi Headstone posted the following comment to an article about this exact thing and it's something everyone needs to consider.

Avatar: Jimi states:
"One thing people are not looking at is this folks, Trumps kid's. Most people say the apple does not fall far from the tree.

Is is not refreshing that in this day and age, his kids are not "kardashian" types by any means? These kids are not in and out of rehab centers, naked pics with boyfriends and girlfriends are not all over the Internet, And think of this...not one news story about these kids. And you know this press corp we have, if any of Trump's kids had a speck of dirt, you would have heard it.

Why is that? In today's America that is unheard of!!!

Trump's Children seem rather respectful don't you think? Take a look at Trump as well, does not drink or smoke, and is in perfect health.

Think too about his employees and confidants. Not one of them has written a tell-all book, publicly denounced him or launched an attack on him. Nobody he's done business with has complained or spoken poorly of him.

So now let's take a look at this story, Glenn Beck on the other hand has had plenty of abuse problems and has some form of mental illness and his business is FAILING. If Glenn Beck could attack Trump's family he would, but guess what? He can't.

There is NOTHING THERE. A wealthy man like Trump with all his ways has children that most Americans would kill for. Even Ted Cruz's wife had some problems. You really have to ponder this point America:

If Trump can succeed with children and a family (including ex-wives) who respect American values, imagine what Trump can do for this country.

A man's values is TRULY judged by his offspring!!!

Feel free to post this where ever you want - this needs attention!! Jimi Headstone"

I do agree, his children impress me, too. They have always impressed me for the very reasons Jimi mentions. They seem highly responsible, decent, respectable. When I look at the children of other very rich people I see spoiled, irresponsible, selfish, immoral young people; but not the Trump Children.

A man who has no respect for women would never be able to raise children like his. Good Job Mr. Trump, you give us all something to strive for.

After that first Fox debate, the gloves came off between Donald Trump and Megyn Kelly and I think we'd all agree, the ordeal was rather nasty. It has dragged into its sixth month now and unfortunately, neither side seems willing to back down.

In the weeks leading up to the highly anticipated second Fox debate, there have been numerous barbs thrown by each side as the war between Kelly and Trump heats up once again.

With the Iowa caucuses only days away, Fox News has escalated their attacks, not only on Mr. Trump but his supporters as well.

Fox host, as well as their guest, have called Trump supporters everything from racist to ignorant but yesterday's press release from Fox News was a new low, even for today's extremely moral-less media standards.

It has become apparent to anyone who's watching that Megyn Kelly has been using her very popular TV show on Fox News as a tool to destroy Mr. Trump. It began on August 6, 2015 with the first debate in Cleveland, Ohio and has continued with this one.

On Tuesday, January 26, 2016, Fox put out the following statement, infuriating not only Mr. Trump but his supporters as well.

I am one of them and when I read it the first time, I actually thought it was some kind of joke, put out there by some sick person trying to create controversy. Then I found out it was really from Fox News and my blood began to boil. I wasn't the only one. Within hours, the comment boards and blogs lit up with angry Trump supporters. They demanded Ms. Kelly be removed, even putting out a petition to have her removed.

The now infamous statement from Fox News last night was a response to a poll Trump put out on Twitter, asking his supporters if he should even attend the debate because we all knew he would be standing before the firing squad. Fox News and Megyn Kelly made their position clear.

The statement put out by Fox said, "We learned from a secret back channel that the Ayatollah and Putin both intend to treat Donald Trump unfairly when they meet with him if he becomes president — a nefarious source tells us that Trump has his own secret plan to replace the Cabinet with his Twitter followers to see if he should even go to those meetings."

The Fox News statement was widely criticized for its hostile tone, especially by anchors on other networks.

"I would tell them to go to hell a lot faster than Donald Trump," said MSNBC's Joe Scarborough earlier this morning, adding that he would rather "set myself on fire" than participate in a debate by a person issuing that statement.

I'm liking Joe Scarborough more and more every day.

That afternoon, Mr. Trump held a press conference in which he gave this response to the childish taunt put out there by Fox News Reps.

Mr. Trump said he was outraged by the "wise guy" remarks. "I didn't like the fact that they sent out press releases toying, talking about Putin, and playing games. I don't know what games Roger Ailes is playing, what's wrong over there? Something's wrong," Trump said. "Let's see how much money Fox is going to make on the debate without me," he added. "It's time that somebody plays grownup."[153]

Trump then announced he would not attend Thursday's debate over his objections to Fox News Channel's anchor and debate moderator Megyn Kelly. "Megyn Kelly's really biased against me," he said in an Instagram video that day. "She knows that. I know that. Everybody knows that. Do you really think she can be fair at a debate?"

I took a deep breath when I heard him say that and even though I agreed with him, I knew the media would say some of the nastiest things about him for this.

Pundits everywhere began predicting the demise of Trump's campaign, once again. They called him a crybaby and accused him of being scared of Megyn Kelly. But Fox News still wanted his attendance very badly. They knew without him, ratings would plummet.

So Wednesday evening before the debate, Fox News executives had Bill O'Reilly beg Trump on "The O'Reilly Factor" to attend the debate. In light of everything that has happened and all that Fox has been exposed of, it was a pathetic display by an otherwise self-confident, diplomatic commentator, Bill O'Reilly.

Donald Trump's appearance on O'Reilly's show that night helped boost the ratings to a two-month high of 3.8 million viewers. Host Bill O'Reilly tried his best to persuade Trump to reconsider and attend the debate.

"You are depriving people of seeing you in a forum they want to see you in," O'Reilly said to Trump before asking him point blank if he'd reconsider. "You and I had an agreement that you would not ask me that," responded Trump.[154] O'Reilly failed.

So instead of doing the Fox Debate, Mr. Trump hosted a live event of his own at the exact same time as the debate. Donald Trump's event was a fund-raiser/rally to raise money for the wounded warriors and veterans.

Like so many other people, if Trump wasn't in the debate, I had no intention of watching it.

Instead I'm watching Trump's live event on YouTube and I am not alone. Right now there are 60,000 viewers on this web channel alone.

Trump takes the stage and says it's like the Academy awards with more cameras then at the Fox Debate. Everyone has bailed on Fox and is watching Trump. Many of the networks have agreed to air Trump's event instead of the debate and there are many websites to stream it from.

Melania is there, as beautiful as always, sitting in the front row. He asks her to stand and she waves to a cheering audience of her husband's fans.

Former Governor Mike Huckabee and Former Senator Rick Santorum are also in attendance. They decided to skip the Fox Debate in lieu of Trump's event because they both love our vets and realized, like Trump, that the Fox Debate is a sham.

Mr. Trump called them both onstage and as usual, each of them gave rousing and patriotic speeches to the rambunctious crowd.

Mike Huckabee said, "Rick Santorum, Donald Trump and I might be competitors in this campaign but tonight we are colleagues in unison…"

He goes on to thank Donald Trump for standing up for our veterans and for allowing him and Rick the opportunity to join him in this project. Mr. Huckabee is a loving, caring man but when I look at him, I don't see a President, I see a tremendous grandfather. I bet his grandkids would say "his hugs are the best".

The event raised over 6 million dollars which is astounding considering they put it together in quick order. Below is a list of where the money came from:

Website Donations	500,000
Carl Icahn	1 million
Richard LeFrak	100,000
Donald J. Trump	1 million
The Fisher Family of NY	75,000
Howard Lauberg	100,000
Anonymous Donor	1 million
Ick Perlmutter	1 million
J.J. Cafaro	50,000
Mr. And Mrs. Phil Ruffin	1 Million

Mr. Ruffin once told his good friend Donald Trump, "If you run for president, I will give you one million dollars." Then Donald announced his run and Mr. Ruffin lived up to his word by sending his friend a million dollar check. Trump sent it back with a no thank you, because unlike any other politician we've ever seen, Donald Trump is self-funding his campaign, so there is no question as to who he works for.

There are many speakers at the event tonight including a green beret named John Wayne Walding, who was born on the Fourth of July and lost his leg in Afghanistan. He once asked his father why they named him John Wayne. His father's reply was, "Well, you were born on a cool day, so you had to have a cool name." Given what he's been through, I'd say, he has definitely lived up to the name. The Legend lives on.

He quickly tells a story that I've heard before; however, many people may not have.

Donald Trump's limousine broke down on the side of the road. Cars just drove past, with no one stopping. After some time, an older couple stopped to help him out, and he was off again. A few days later, Mr. Trump tracked them down and paid off their mortgage. This is just the kind of man he is. Generous without seeking merit.

Mr. Walding gives a moving speech of what it's like to be a veteran. Losing his legs was a low point for him and he knows what it's like to see your life changed in the blink of an eye.

He tells what it was like for our Vietnam Vets who were called "baby killers" and spit on when they got home or what it's like to have to look at the faces of the families as their loved ones ride home in a coffin with our beautiful American flag draped on top. He describes the sadness that comes with the job of a soldier. He praises the fallen, especially the 22 who lose their lives every day.

He tells what it means to hear the words "Thank you" from Americans, to which he replies "you were worth it". That made me cry because my son is a soldier.

He talks about the #22KILL movement which is a global movement created by veterans with a mission to:

Honor those who serve or served.

Raise awareness to veteran suicide and mental health issues such as PTSD and TBI.

Educate the public about current veteran-related topics and issues.

Recruit veteran advocates aka "Battle Buddies" and support various veteran empowerment programs; i.e. Honor Courage Commitment, Inc. (HCC), Equest Hooves for Heroes, Carrick Brain Center, UTD Center for BrainHealth, REACT, Adaptive Training Foundation, and more.

If you are interested in becoming a 22KILL Certified organization please email them at 22KILL@veteran.me.

Honor Courage Commitment, Inc. started the #22KILL movement in 2013 after learning about the staggering statistic that an average of 22 veterans are killed, by their own hands, every day.

They wear a ring, the "Honor Ring™", on their trigger fingers for a reason, not as a fashion statement but a life statement, because as they know, every life lost is devastating to us as a nation but the ring also represents the poor souls and their families for their sacrifices and their loss.

The Honor Ring is a black band worn on the index finger as a "silent salute" to all veterans, past and present. This ring is a symbol of respect and simply says that you support those who have served our military. The #22KILL program is also a reminder to veterans and veteran supporters that they are never alone; that we are all family.

Mr. Walding is joined on the stage with representatives from the organization and together they present Mr. Trump with his very own Honor Ring.

Diamond and Silk then join Mr. Trump on stage. They are immediately met with protesters, who are met with Trump supporters, who are much louder than the quickly silenced protesters.

These women are energetic fighters and they "love them some Trump". Their videos are an Internet sensation that often go viral and apparently Mr. Trump loves them, too

Trump then goes into full campaign mode, finishing with his patriotic call for all for us to help him "Make America Great Again".

Within 24 hours, the Trump organization managed to put together an amazing event for our veterans and raise more than six million dollars for 22 charities at the same time.

But this event wasn't just for the veterans, it was also for me and you and every American who loves our country. It was emotionally charged and made me proud to be an American once again.

Great job Donald Trump! Just imagine what a President Trump could do for you.

I wonder how many watched the Fox News Debate. I can't wait to get that number tomorrow morning.

Many supporters, myself included, have been quite concerned that the events of the past few weeks might damage the candidate we are supporting. After reading the comments of multiple publications and blogs, that doesn't seem to be the case.

Comments from the People on Breitbart Live Updates website were very telling.[155] Here are just a few:

Avatar: Ann
"Tonight will be remembered as the night when national television FINALLY turned to one central and crucial message: EVERY SINGLE veteran of the 22 killing themselves each day is one death TOO MANY, one totally UNNECESSARY death, and as a country it is our DUTY to prevent this from happening.

If you have fought for America, the one thing you DESERVE most is to LIVE, and to know that no matter what, YOU did more than 99% of the American people, to make America great again, EVEN if at times you didn't agree with the political choices of the Commander in Chief who has been your boss.

It's BECAUSE the military RESPECTS elections that this country has known so many moments of greatness, and will continue to do so.

America CONTINUES to need you. All you have to do is find out how.

Thank you Trump, for making it possible to have all the media focus on something like this.

And thanks Huckabee and Santorum for knowing when it's time to put America first!"

Avatar: Ginger Li responded:
"As Pat Caddell said, there's insurgency in the air i.e. rebellion. For so long, the powers that be dictate behavior via Political Correctness and

media/educational indoctrination. No one has been willing to question or challenge the rules of engagement until Trump. We are being subjected to an orchestrated invasion and told to shut up if we object to it. Meanwhile the DC rats are consuming everything in sight. The citizen anger is bubbling to the surface and finding expression in the Trump candidacy. And tonight, the media was told to sit on it - we're taking back our political process. It's as simple as that."

Avatar: ArmchairNinja began this thread:
"If Donald Trump hadn't put his foot down, NONE of this tough talk would have happened."

Avatar: Anat T. to ArmchairNinja:
Key sentence above, in support of what you say:
"It appears as though the candidates have figured out that standing up to Fox News is suddenly pretty popular with voters."
Though it should be "standing up to the entire media establishment". I call it "Palin's revenge".

Avatar: YUGE to Anat T:
"The Palin Endorsement (Master Persuader Series).
In the 2D world of traditional politics, Sarah Palin's endorsement of Donald Trump looks like a yawn because she's seen by many as a policy lightweight. But in the 3D world of persuasion, where Trump lives, it is probably a home-run."
DONALD J. TRUMP FOR PRESIDENT

Avatar: Marie Joseph to ArmchairNinja:

"Trump is my favorite Republican shit-starter. He's okay by me for attacking the structures and organizations like Fox that have undue influence on the elections and in shaping public opinion. Media should simply report on elections and politicians, not try to manage the political process. Wish one of our candidates in the Democratic party would do this!" END OF THREAD.

Avatar: Hawkeye:
"There is NO law that says a political candidates MUST take orders from the MSM OR take part in any debates. THAT is strictly his or her prerogative. If this works for Trump then he ends up bigger and stronger than ever before and he's the political genius his supporters think he is. It is, after all, HIS gamble and HIS consequences. IF it backfires then all his critics will celebrate his having to deal with the backlash, and again, that's on HIM. I applaud his putting the networks in their place. They've been unchallenged king makers and breakers for FAR too long. Trump has had to put up with being MOCKED by these A-Holes and THAT should NEVER happen coming from an INDUSTRY that is, after all, supposed to serve a necessary need for the Public, NOT themselves. I guess even THEY have to admit by now that TRUMP is a SERIOUS contender to Obama's Throne. It's about TIME that these debates get back to being about the Candidates and NOT about the Moderators looking for HIT points as was the case with that fat a**ed Candy Crowley."

Avatar: artlett2015:

"Oh so glad Trump is Calling Fox out. The Media thinks they "rule" who will be elected President. God I love it; Trump is so gutsy and unique. No one like him. The GOP establishment looks so boring, big Stiffs, all talk, and have betrayed the American People over and over. If I hear Rubio talk about his maid mother again, I think I will Scream!"

Avatar: JMGL:
"Mr. Trump, stand your ground and don't back down to anyone. I love that "Screw you" spirit. TRUMP 2016"

Avatar: Tommy Hoffmann:
"This is a master-stroke by Trump. He will put together a nationally-televised fundraiser for Veterans and run it up against the debate. He's so damn smart he's certainly thought of this already, but it will be commercial-free so people don't switch over to the debate during the ads.

The next day and all weekend the contrast will be made between Trump supporting the veterans and the Seven Dwarfs trying to bash Trump during a debate no one watched. Absolutely brilliant!"

Avatar: 55369:
"Donald Trump will still dominate the debate. References to Donald trump will be abundant. Trump supporters will be there for him and boo the negative responses. The others will be doing their best to destroy Trump.

Arrogant stupidity will be front and center. Watch for all of the untruths to be spoken being there will be no immediate response to set the record straight."

Avatar: ksst replied to 55369:
"But we, the Trump supporters will show up in those overnight polls. They will see that the absent candidate wins the debate, how will that look to the rest of the clowns?"

Avatar: pismopal:
"Funny how Fox characterizes the absence of Trump as "fear" of Kelly. Speaking of presidents and meeting other world leaders, no world leader is going to attend a meeting that is obviously an ambush."

Avatar: Rob Nashdroid:
"Trump has nothing to lose: he's brilliant. Odds are that the ratings will fall significantly for Fox, thus increasing Fox's reckless hatred of Trump, thus making Trump even more appealing to regular voters and cementing his "independent and beholden-to-no-one" image. And it gets even better: I heard that Trump is going to host a fundraiser for wounded veterans at the same time as the debate! This will draw CNN and MSNBC over to Trump's event. Trump is a genius!"

Avatar: Andrew writes:
"Like him or not, it's great to see a candidate tell the establishment to go to hell, when appropriate. For too long have these mainstream media platforms held too much sway over election outcomes. Well played

on this one, Mr. Trump! Good luck with your veterans' event, Sir."

Avatar: Theo:
"Trump is playing a deeper game here than anyone realizes. Trump is a master of marketing and thus of mass psychology. The target of his messaging isn't the media or the political establishment; it's the voting public, especially the Iowans at the moment. This is a psychological ploy aimed at voters, not just a power play aimed at the media.

The Iowa Caucuses are notoriously unpredictable. Iowans love defying the polls, so Trumps polling leads aren't as helpful going into the caucuses as most people might think.

Trump has now set up a confrontation between himself and the rest of the field by holding his own show directly opposite the Fox News debate. The victor of this contest will be measured by ratings, not polls, and it will be Trump.

This will give Trump extra momentum going into the caucuses. It will allow Trump's people in the caucuses to make the argument that Iowa has the opportunity to back a winner for once. Iowa can play king maker, instead of just "shaping the race".

Iowa can give the clear winner the momentum to "run the table", or it can be left behind again. Best of all, even if Trump doesn't win the caucuses, he will be able to point to beating the rest of the field (and beating Fox News) via the debate ploy, and have that momentum going into NH."

Avatar: JBO believes:

"FOX NEWS GETS SERIOUS REALITY CHECK".

"A once arrogant network, expecting to be the mouthpiece for the republican establishment for the next four years, received a rude awakening this week. Counting on a new 'king maker' role, FOX soon found out that they are an unessential part in the 2016 GOP Presidential Primary."

And last but certainly not least is *buzman* who stated rather crudely but accurately:

Avatar: buzman,
"Trump travels in a 757 jet since it's the only jet capable of carrying his balls around the country. BOYCOTT FOX, TRUMP 2016 !!!!!"

Donald J. Trump can do almost anything he wants and the people will still love him because it is truly "An American Love-Fest".

A TRUMP-LESS DEBATE

Last night's Republican presidential debate generated a much smaller viewership than anticipated by Fox. It actually came in as the second least watched debate thus far, according to preliminary Nielsen estimates.

I had to Google exactly how the Nielsen ratings work, but in a nutshell, Nielsen ratings are a measurement of the audience, used to determine size and composition of television consumers in the U.S. Market.

The overnight metered-market represent 56 of the nation's largest markets and they gave the Fox News debate in Iowa last night an 8.4 household rating in that market.

The most recent GOP debate on Fox Business Network was held earlier this month and received a 7.4 overnight rating making last night's debate the second lowest-rated of the six Republican debates this cycle.

Nielsen will issue its official viewership numbers later today, but the preliminary count shows that the debate on Fox last night averaged in the vicinity of 12 million viewers. That number is exactly half of the number from the first debate in which Wallace, Baier and Kelly also moderated.

Curiosity over an unpredictable Trump, fueled record tune-in for the first GOP debate last summer, as Fox News Channel drew 24 million in Cleveland, the largest ever audience for a non-sports cable program. CNN followed that up a month later with a little over 23 million viewers for their debate. Ratings dipped for the subsequent four debates, ranging between 11.1 million and 18.2 million, though those numbers are still higher than in previous years.

The Democratic debates have rated even lower viewership, but at least some of that is due to three of them being scheduled in low-profile time-slots on the weekend. One in particular was scheduled at the same time as a football game on the eve of a holiday. Not many watched that one, as was the hope of the DNC. Their main objective right now is to keep Hillary Clinton hidden as much as possible. They realize that she isn't a strong candidate but she is their "Chosen One" and they'll do anything to ensure her coronation.

And no matter how much Bernie Sanders complains about that, the DNC always manages to straighten him out, with a cookie and a warm glass of milk.

Avatar: timentide:
"Trump has shined a spotlight on one of Washington's best kept secrets: namely, Fox's role via its founder Rupert Murdoch in pushing an open borders agenda. The Trump campaign is a direct threat to Murdoch's efforts to open America's borders. Well-concealed from virtually all reporting on Fox's treatment of Trump is the fact that Murdoch is the co-chair of what is arguably one of the most powerful immigration lobbying firms in country, the Partnership for a New American Economy (PNAE)."
"The Trump campaign is a direct threat to Murdoch's efforts to open America's borders."
Megyn Kelly is Murdock's puppet and attack dog sent out to destroy Donald Trump because he is a threat to Rupert Murdock's anti-American agenda.
Fair and balanced? You decide. Trump 2016 - 20!!!!"

Avatar: SonsofLiberty7676:
"TRUMP breaks every rule in the Establishment book! FOX says you have to attend debate or lose presidency- He says scr*w you- I reach more people and take tougher questions everyday! FOX says in the end we will control the process-
TRUMP says-No The people do!"

Avatar: FickleFinger:

"Rupert Murdoch, get your hands off our country's future. You can't dictate to us what is good for us. Take your Wall Street Journal and Fox News and shove them where the sun don't shine. If we want secure borders, we, the American people, WILL have secure borders and you can just continue to be an impotent old curmudgeon with money."

Avatar: timentide:
"The only reason Murdock became an American citizen was to enrich himself and further his globalist agenda. If it has his fingerprints on it it stinks. The extent he has gone to to destroy Trump's campaign because Trump was a threat to Murdock's global open borders agenda shows he is a very dangerous man. Forget about the pretenders, Trump has shown he is the only one who will stand up to this flea.
Trump 2016!!!"

Avatar: Anonymous:
"My fellow Americans, THIS is what we are up against! It's the globalists and their candidates (you should know who they are by now), versus American Citizens and our Constitution. Bad enough we have to endure the United Nations, but Globalists such as Murdock (and Soros) are the biggest threat. BOYCOTT FOX NOW!"

Avatar: Elaine:
"Wow! this does clear things up. We kept wondering why Fox people slammed Trump, every chance they had. Trump stuck to his guns & this proves him right. He kept saying that there were

people at Fox that were/are unfair to him. Trump called it. He forced Ailes' & Murdoch's hand & he will do the same in DC!!"

WHO WON THE DEBATE? THE POLLS KNOW

The first polls are in and it looks like our very own, Donald J. Trump, has won another debate. And this time, he wasn't even there!

The Drudge Report 2016 On-line Poll located at www.drudge.com, showed the following results to the question "Who won the debate?"

TRUMP	57.36%	(155,315 votes)
CRUZ	20.22%	(54,743 votes)
RUBIO	8.16%	(22,097 votes)
PAUL	7.76%	(21,017 votes)
CARSON	1.36%	(3,694 votes)
KASICH	1.32%	(3,587 votes)
CHRISTIE	1.14%	(3,097 votes)
BUSH	1.09%	(2,942 votes)
FIORINA	1.03%	(2,791 votes)
SANTORUM	0.29%	(772 votes)
HUCKABEE	0.27%	(723 votes)

Total Votes Cast: 270,778

The NJ.com also known as True Jersey, had their on-line poll located at: www.nj.com.

The poll question was: Who won the Republican presidential debate tonight? And the result are:

Donald Trump	64.56%	(1,461 votes)
Rand Paul	10.91%	(247 votes)
Marco Rubio	7.51%	(170 votes)
Ted Cruz	6.01%	(136 votes)
John Kasich	3.27%	(74 votes)
Chris Christie	3.27%	(74 votes)
I don't know.	1.94%	(44 votes)

Jeb Bush   1.59% (36 votes)
Ben Carson   .93%   (21 votes)
          Total Votes Cast: 2,263

Slate.com, located at http://www.slate.com, asked the poll participants the same question as the other two. Who won the debate?

Donald Trump   45%
Rand Paul   18%
Marco Rubio   13%
Ted Cruz   9%
John Kasich   5%
Ben Carson   3%
Chris Christie   3%
Jeb Bush   2%
Carly Fiorina   2%
Mike Huckabee   1%
          Total Votes Cast: Unknown

Time Magazine polled their readers "Who won the debate?" at www.time.com

Donald Trump   53 %
Rand Paul   19 %
Marco Rubio   12 %
Ted Cruz   7 %
Jeb Bush   4 %
Chris Christie   2 %
John Kasich   2 %
Ben Carson   1 %
          Total Votes Cast: 41,177

The Blaze at www.theblaze.com, asked this question:

Who Won the Iowa Fox News Debate?

Donald Trump	51 %
Ted Cruz	24 %
Rand Paul	10 %
Marco Rubio	9 %
Ben Carson	2 %
Jeb Bush	1 %
John Kasich	1 %
Chris Christie	1 %
Carly Fiorina	1 %
Rick Santorum	0 %
Mike Huckabee	0 %
Jim Gilmore	0 %

Total Votes Cast: 120,753

All morning, I've been looking for the official viewer ratings for the Fox debate last night, but can't seem to find it. It must not be a good number because Fox News didn't waste any time posting the 24 million viewers that watched their first debate. So where's the number Fox News?

Roger Ailes is sweating bullets today, desperately trying to quell some of the damage done to his network.

This commenter below explains what happened very well.

Avatar: Ewww
"To those who think the right wing media is fair and balanced:

We see that Fox News bias their debates in two ways. The first is by promoting candidates that have ties to their operations, such as the case for Marco

Rubio. The second is that they seem to always have a candidate 'push' ready, such as "gotcha" media where they challenge people on a previous statement.

But in no case do they allow the viewer a fair shot. Historically in debates, candidates were asked to explain their position on particular points, with each being asked the same question. It allowed us to compare and contrast each subject, weighing the response to how we feel about a particular topic. Those days are gone.

The same holds for Glenn Beck and the Blaze. Glenn no longer presents just facts to let us judge. He is openly involved in attempting to sway the vote in favor of a candidate he likes. In this case it is Ted Cruz, who employs millionaire directors within his campaign, such as the real estate tycoon director running the anti-abortion positions.

All of these people suffer the same delusional status. They love to elbow with the wealthy, and in the case of Beck you have someone with an estimated $250m portfolio valuation hob-knobbing with other millionaires. Or Megan Kelly who believes she is now more important and righteous than the truth.

I feel sad for both Glenn and Megan. The very values that made them successful have been transgressed, and they both feel they are now king makers. Yet to both I cite a simple adage, it's easier to pass through the eye of a needle.

You may both be O.K. with your wealth and fame induced maladaptive views. But there will be a judgment, and the Lord knows their hearts.

How is Glenn or Megan now any different than the pundits on the liberal side of the news? They no longer are, they are the same. Only the names are changed to promote their audience and wealth."

Avatar: Gary More is hopeful:
"The people have already chosen their next president, voting is just a formality now."

Avatar: WillNotBeFooledByObamaNATION:
"So many KOOL-AID DRINKERS AND DEMONRATS Bashing Mr. Donald Trump for boycotting the debate and calling him all kinds of names. YOU ARE MORONS AND FOAMING IN YOUR MOUTH. Just look at the POLLS, 83% of VIEWERS are in concert with what the DONALD is doing and the HEADLINES TOMORROW WILL READ LIKE THIS… Drudge poll results should be hilarious.
Trump skips debate. Trump wins debate."

Avatar: Ann:
"I love the Trump kids. Yes, the Romney kids were also very classy, but at the same time, they constantly came across as distant, cold elitists, just like their father, whereas the Trump kids are truly modest and warm and charming, and everybody knows they are working really hard, and constantly meeting a lot of different people, from all walks of life, just like their father.
You cannot possibly be, as a person, all that people are throwing at Trump since he started to run for president, if THIS is how you managed to educate your own children, EVEN when you had to go through a divorce, by the way.

Now, let's stop the silly debates and start taking care of our veterans!"

IT'S CRUNCH TIME

Donald Trump is having a rally today in Nassau, N.H. to a packed audience, full of energy and eager to be a part of the love-fest for Mr. Trump.

He takes the stage to adoring fans, cheering amongst a sea of Trump banners, hats and waving flags.

He says "Last night was amazing, we raised 6 million dollars for our vets." and the crowd goes wild.

Mr. Trump admits that boycotting the Fox News Debate was risky but it seems to have worked out well for the campaign and the veterans. And he's right, he's dominating all of the news cycles today.

Donald Trump and Senator Ted Cruz have been in a consistent tie for weeks in the battle to win Iowa. But this morning, Trump once again has a decent lead going into the Iowa caucus. He's in a terrific position to run the table, winning every one of the first states.

He loves to talk about the polls and is about to now. He is often asked, "Why do you talk about the polls so much?" His quirky reply was quite simple. "Because I'm number one, you're not." And it's true. Donald Trump has remained number one in nearly every poll taken since the day he announced his run in June of 2015.

His rallies break records for venues, some long held by rock stars. I've never seen any candidate draw crowds like Trump does in a primary. Other than

Barack Obama, I can't remember a candidate so loved by the people.

At almost every rally, Donald Trump describes what he sees as a "love-fest". Reporters write about the people's love affair with this man. They can't understand it, but for those of us who feel it, it's an amazing thing, this American Love-Fest.

It's two days before the first caucus in Iowa and Donald Trump will not be leaving the state until the caucus is over and the votes are counted.

MARSHALLTOWN, IOWA

Craig Z. of Marshalltown has voted for Democrats all his life, including twice for President Barack Obama, but not this year. He's switching his party so he can vote for Donald Trump and I'll let him tell you why.

"The whole country is going to hell," the 66-year-old retired factory worker said, standing against the bleachers at a high school gymnasium while waiting for Republican presidential candidate Donald Trump to arrive.

His anger is like all of ours, "Roads and bridges in the U.S. are falling apart, jobs are scarce and the U.S. border is wide open." he says.

"We're letting all these people into the country. No one even knows who the hell they are," he said. "We don't need any more Arabs. The United States, anymore, is just a dumping ground for everyone."

Craig plans to caucus for a Republican on Monday, likely for Trump because he says that Trump is, "the only one with brains."

Obama's 2008 campaign defined the election as one of "hope and change," however, this year's election can be said to be built on rage.

In the surveys I received from many potential voters of both parties, I found that anger and rebellion were the driving motivator of this election cycle.

The People are fed up with Washington career politicians who seem to work only two or three days a week and get very little accomplished aside from raising money for their upcoming campaigns. They're angry about their decreased wages, about companies sending their jobs overseas and they are terrified because it is common knowledge that terrorists are sneaking in across the border. It is even common knowledge that the Obama administration is actively bringing them in through the Migrant program. The fear and rage are both real and they are driving the campaigns of the "outsiders."

For Republican voters, the outsiders are the ever bombastic Donald Trump and his second closest competitor, Senator Ted Cruz.

I have been to two Trump rallies myself but I have watched every single one of them on YouTube. I can attest, they are energetic events. There are often times protesters in the audience but once they get started, Trump supporters take them down with their chants of "Trump, Trump, Trump" while Mr. Trump urges his security to "get them the hell out of here."

Trump has been heard telling his security to "confiscate the coat of a protester." Of course, we all know it was in jest but it was met with tremendous audience approval as they cheered and chanted "USA,

USA, USA, USA". Trump rallies are always loads of fun.

Donald Trump has more energy than anyone I've ever seen. He has three separate rallies scheduled in one day in Iowa. The first one, in Dubuque has just begun with a speaker explaining the caucus process.

When he's finished, he asks the crowd, "Who is going to caucus Monday evening?". The crowd cheers. He then asks, "Who is going to caucus for Mr. Trump?" and the crowd goes wild. Lastly, he asks, "Who is going to bring 25 of their friends to caucus for Mr. Trump?" Nearly every banner flies as the crowd professes their loyalty to Donald Trump.

To the delight of the crowd, he throws "Make America Great Again" hats into the masses until he is completely out of breath. Then he once again implores them to get out and caucus and wear their hats when they do.

Mr. Trump has an amazing ground game and as I was perusing his current schedule of events on his website www.donaldjtrump.com, I was amazed to see that in the next ten days, he has twelve rallies scheduled. Who can keep up that pace? Our next President, that's who.

Mr. Trump arrives at the airport in his beautiful Trump jet. The crowd erupts in cheers as their hero quickly descends the stairs to join them on the tarmac

He walks to the podium, with a bounce in his step, because Donald Trump has more energy than anyone I've ever seen.

He talks for a few minutes, then asks "Are there are any kids in the audience around the age of ten?".

Many hands are raised. He then tells the children to head over there, pointing off to the side, because he's going to let them run through his jet for a few minutes. But "no parents allowed because adults tend to make too many messes' Trump said to the delighted children. They quickly abandon their parents for a chance to see inside that amazingly beautiful airplane.

As the children have the time of their lives, something they'll remember forever, Mr. Trump talks to their parents and other supporters, in one last attempt to secure their votes.

The polls today reflect very good news for Mr. Trump. The Real Clear Politics poll[156] is one of the leading polls in the industry. It reflects an average of the top polls for the day.

Today it shows that Donald Trump is again leading Senator Ted Cruz in Iowa by 6 points, with 48 hours to go.

Avatar: Ken:
"Just listening to the news, looking at the polls being released, and looking at all the positive excitement surrounding Trump. It is easy to come to that conclusion.

Maybe just the fact he has the lead in every national poll since he entered the race might give one a slim clue."

Avatar: TheSuperPatriot replied to Ken:
"Still rising in Iowa. Still in the lead."

Avatar: trepan:

"Can't wait till Iowa... when Trump wins by a landslide, the establishment will implode..."

THE IOWA CAUCUS

Tonight is the night we've all been waiting for. I'm sitting in front of my laptop, nervous but hopeful. All the final polling numbers look great for Donald Trump. But as we all know, it's not over until the fat lady sings.

At 2:35 pm today Facebook released their "search numbers"[157] and they were quite interesting. It seems that Bernie Sanders Google searches and Donald Trump were the most discussed topics when it came to the candidates in Iowa today. The breakdown was this:

Sanders:	42.2%
Trump:	21.7%
Clinton:	13.1%
Cruz:	10.7%
Paul:	4.7%
Carson:	2.6%
Rubio:	1.9%

The increase in Bernie Sanders searches is mostly due to the recent events coming out about Hillary Clinton. Up until this point, most Democrat Iowans were leaning toward Clinton, but Democrats are worried about her electability and are looking to the lesser of two evils, Mr. Bernie Sanders, as their alternative to Mrs. Clinton.

I'm trolling the comments on various websites while listening to Newsmax Live TV at www.newsmaxtv.com. They will be airing live until the last vote is counted.

Right now they are taking calls from the public and in call after call, I hear support for Donald Trump.

There are millions of people, just like me, who are glued to their keyboards, sweating it out. We are all just looking for a sign, any sign of what's to come.

Twitter followers in Iowa began tweeting from the caucus lines, attempting to keep the rest of America informed. These are some of their tweets:

Ben Jacobs ✔*@Bencjacobs* tweeted out about a fellow caucus goer:

"Deborah Humphrey is at her caucus to support Trump. She says she last voted in 1968 for Richard Nixon"

7:26 PM - 1 Feb 2016

7:34 PM *scottinankeny* commented on a message board:

"In line waiting to caucus #IowaCaucus huge turnout - weather not an issue in Des Moines"

7:36 PM *@BradAndersonIA* tweeted:

"Sweaty packed gym. Turnout intense at Perkins Elementary."

7:36 PM *@RichardDedor* was short but to the point:

"Wow. Unreal turnout!"

7:36 PM *Jennifer Jacobs* ✔*@JenniferJJacobs*
"Crazy amounts of new registrations at GOP caucuses, longtime activists tell me"

7:48 PM *Ben Jacobs* ✔*@Bencjacobs*
"I am at a Republican caucus on the east side of Des Moines, Democratic leaning blue collar area. There is huge turnout here"

7:57 PM *John Nichols@NicholsUprising*
"Very large turnout on north side of Des Moines for caucuses. Lots of young people. Lots of 1st-timers."

7:59 PM *Josh Kraushaar@HotlineJosh*
"Dallas Co GOP chair Trevor de Haan announces precinct has already set record turnout with 10 minutes left to go"

8:02 PM *Maggie Haberman* ✔*@maggieNYT*
"Trump is appearing at a caucus site in West Des Moines with huge turnout"

8:32 PM POLITICO ✔*@politico*
"Huge crowds are overwhelming caucus organizers at precincts across Iowa http://politi.co/1PbFmEj| AP Photo"

8:20 PM *John King* ✔*@JohnKingCNN*
"One Scott County GOP site that had 19 voters 2012 has more than 100. At#*ISU*- GOP site expecting 100 or so has maybe 800."

8:23 PM *FiveThirtyEight* ✔*@FiveThirtyEight*
"Entrance polls have Donald Trump narrowly leading on the Republican side"

Unfortunately, the entrance polls were wrong because Donald Trump finished second to Ted Cruz.

The media described it as a humiliating defeat, claiming that Donald Trump had lost the race, therefore he's lost his mojo. All the while, claiming the third place victor, Marco Rubio did an amazing job.

How is it, that a second place win is a loss but third place is a win? Our biased main stream media, that's how. They'll do anything to cast doubt in the eyes of Trump supporters. Little do they realize, we are on to them.

TED CRUZ CAMPAIGN CAUGHT CHEATING

There is a disturbing turn of events coming out of Iowa today as Dr. Ben Carson and his campaign have just accused Senator Ted Cruz's team of cheating in order to win. Cruz and his team were caught trying to sabotage Carson in the Iowa caucuses Monday night by telling lies about Dr. Ben Carson. The Cruz camp was telling voters that Dr. Carson was leaving the race after Iowa and that they shouldn't waste their vote. They should vote for Ted Cruz instead of Carson.

"It was happening all over," Iowa State Director Ryan Rhodes told MSNBC.

Even Ben Carson's own wife, Candy Carson, heard the rumors as she walked in to the caucus precinct in Alkeny. Mrs. Carson actually took to the podium and gave an impromptu speech to the crowd in order to correct the record, telling voters that "it was all a lie." Carson won the precinct that his wife was at because she was able to get the truth out, but the damage was done. Carson only made it to fourth place in the Iowa caucuses.

When the media confronted the Cruz campaign about the allegations by Carson, the Cruz spokesman Rick Tyler denied them but did admit that his people did alert some supporters that Carson planned to go to Florida after the Iowa caucuses instead of campaigning.

Carson's campaign did say he was going home for just 24 hours before returning to the campaign trail, but never did he say he was quitting the race.

Carson told reporters earlier in the night that he planned to go to Florida for a day to get "fresh clothes" after 18 days on the campaign trail, pushing back against "false media reports" that Carson was suspending his campaign.

But one prominent Cruz surrogate, Rep. Steve King, took that snippet of information and ran with it. King sent a tweet describing Carson's move as a sign the retired pediatric neurosurgeon was getting out of the race.

Before long, the Cruz campaign was calling it's local staff informing them that Carson was dropping out and that they should tell Carson voters to vote for Cruz instead.

"That's really quite a dirty trick," Carson told reporters later that evening, "I want my supporters to recognize this makes me more determined than ever to keep going."

To have the Cruz campaign send emails to their caucus speakers suggesting that Dr. Carson was doing anything but moving forward after tonight is the sleaziest of tactics in American politics. It's outright theft of votes and because of it, Carson lost.

Carson's state co-chair, Rob Taylor, was more blunt in his condemnation of the Cruz camps actions, saying "This is horses—t, bottom line. You can bleep it out all you want, but Iowans understand," added Taylor.

A half dozen Iowans, many of then connected with MSNBC by the Carson campaign, told stories of being mislead about Carson's intentions in the race.

Barb Heki, a home-school activist and Gov. Mike Huckabee supporter who said she is friendly with nearly all the campaigns in Iowa, told MSNBC that the speakers supporting Cruz at her caucus location, Hyperion Point Country Club in Johnston, Iowa, announced that Carson was getting out of the race before several-hundred caucus-goers as her location took a vote.

"They gave their speech for Ted Cruz and said we also need to announce, and let you know, that Dr. Ben Carson has announced that he's suspending his race for awhile after the caucuses are over," Heki said.

Some Cruz supporters confirmed that the campaign had alerted them, however Tyler denied this, stating that they'd only told voters that Carson was going home after Iowa.

Pam Westrum was also at the caucus site with Heki and said she was "really rattled" when Cruz supporters said Carson had gotten out of the race, while Lisa Greenwood was the precinct speaker for Carson at a caucus site at Iowa State University when the Cruz speaker asked her to support the Texas senator because Carson was dropping out of the race. She said she was very confused, but caucused for Carson nonetheless.

In Waterloo, Iowa, Kim Murray said her caucus leader had told them Carson had dropped out, but did not say where she'd gotten that information; when she saw the votes tallied after the caucus, Carson received only one vote.

Rita Davenport, a Carson campaign volunteer who was her precinct's speaker in Boone, Iowa said she'd also been told by Cruz supporters that Carson was dropping out.

"Something just really crazy happened here in Iowa," Davenport told MSNBC.[158]

During an appearance on the FOX Business Network's 'After the Bell,' Dr. Ben Carson responded to an apology from Ted Cruz, by saying, "As Christians, of course we accept people's apologies, but we also have to ask ourselves is this acceptable to us, the American people, or should there be some accountability?" Carson added: "There should be some consequences for things. You don't just say 'oh, okay, sorry... okay let's move on.' The damage was done to me, it wasn't done to them.[159]"

Sarah Palin had this to say on her Facebook page about the Cruz cheating scandal:

"Dirty Politics: Witnessing Firsthand It's Always Heartbreaking, Never Surprising"

Donald Trump has opened so many people's eyes to the lies, corruption and total lack of accountability that seems to come so naturally to the permanent political class.

I remember hearing a young Senator Ted Cruz say on more than one occasion, that "millions of Americans are asking for accountability and truth."

Which is why the sleazy politics that the Cruz campaign is dabbling in is all the more disturbing to the electorate. Whether you support Ted Cruz or not, I think we can all admit, we really expected better from him than this. It saddens us all that Ted Cruz has decided to walk in the steps of the corrupt elite without any expectation of accountability.

The Obama administration has suffered scandal after scandal, yet no one is every held accountable for their actions. The American people are sick and tired of abuse being heaped on them by their representatives and we are even more sick of no one but us, the people, suffering for their misdeeds. This is why "the status quo has got to go."

The Cruz Campaign's actions to destroy Ben Carson's efforts to serve are no different than Obama's practice of not holding anyone accountable. Typical politics. Typical politicians and a good, decent man, Ted Cruz, has now been compromised.

But the controversy didn't stop there, it actually started when voters in Iowa began receiving official looking letters from their government in the days before the caucus.

The letters actually came from the Ted Cruz Campaign.

It seems Cruz will employ any tactic necessary to win. He sent out fliers that looked like official documents from the state admonishing voters for poor voting records in the past, complete with a "grade" of "A to F", based on your voting history. It also showed the names and grades of their neighbors. The letter also told the receiver that his neighbors were getting the same letter with his name on it but if they went to vote for Ted Cruz, this problem would go away. This is called "vote shaming".

Cruz is a lawyer. Personally, I have seen all I need to see from a lawyer running the White House these past seven years. The joke about trusting lawyers is no longer a joke in today's world. They are the most unethical, plea dealing, corrupt professionals in the working class today, at lease in my humble opinion.

Cruz was always my second choice, until this all happened. Now I see him as just another lying, corrupt politician. He will do nothing as President to provide Americans with jobs, nor will he attempt to get jobs that will make us competitive in the world market. Further, I believe, as do many, Cruz will do nothing about the illegal immigrants taking over our country and taking what few jobs there are away from citizen who need them desperately.

In addition, Ted Cruz seems to knows little about how to deal with our messed up national policies and he certainly can't negotiate with anyone, not even members of his own party, because he is and always has been part of the problem.

In light of current events, if Cruz is the nominee, I am afraid many voters may not vote at all, almost insuring a Democrat win.

Avatar: Esbea writes:
"The words are coming out of Ted's mouth, but given that those who went to caucus for Carson likely pushed Cruz to the win, I doubt he is sorry. If you look

at the tweets put out, his campaign cherry picked one out of a set of 3 that clearly said Carson wasn't leaving the race. Look for no consequences at the Cruz camp. Carson is right about one thing, we are sick of people in power manipulating the system and getting away with it. Just one more reason to distrust Ted."

Avatar: Green_E_Meanie
"All I've been hearing about Cruz by commenters on NewsMax is what a perfect, pure as the wind driven snow, holier than thou Christian he (Cruz) is. A true model of constitutional conservatism they say. Some even went as far as to say God has blessed Ted Cruz and will only bless our country if he is elected.

What a load a crap. The man runs one helluva dirty, dishonest campaign (misleading campaign fliers, Steve Kings lies, Canadian birth, Chicago hacks etc). It sure looks like Cruz is a lot more lawyer and politician than Christian to me; using any means necessary to win.

Thank goodness Iowa is over and we can get on to parts of the country with less hypocritical bible thumpers.

I'll stick with my man, Donald Trump, who is who he says he is, says what he means, does what he says, and is funding his campaign all on his own.

Enjoy your ill begotten 1 electoral vote lead while it lasts, Canadian Ted.. btw is your victory speech over yet? Sheesh TRUMP 2016"

Governor Terry Branstad has credited Ted Cruz with running an "old-fashioned", 99-county campaign which yielded him a slight victory in Monday night's

Iowa Caucuses, but Branstad is joining the chorus criticizing Cruz for "questionable" campaign tactics.

"This thing that they distributed on Caucus night saying that Dr. Carson was likely to drop out and his supporters should support Cruz, that is, I think, unethical and unfair," Branstad said this morning. "I think there'll be repercussions to that."

"You know, we have a strong sense of fairness in Iowa," Branstad said during an interview with Radio Iowa. "Distributing information that was not true about a candidate right at the time people are voting in the Caucuses is an inappropriate thing."

Branstad attended his precinct caucus Monday night, but is not revealing who he voted for. Branstad said the record turn-out he witnessed for Mondays Republican Caucuses was "an encouraging sign" for the fall election, since Iowa is likely to be a toss-up state in the presidential race.[160]

Why is all this important, you might ask. The math tells the story. There are approximately 1500 caucus precincts in Iowa and the final numbers showed that a mere 6239 votes separated Senator Ted Cruz in first place and Donald J. Trump in second.

If what Ted Cruz did to Dr. Carson cost the neurosurgeon as little as 4.15 votes per precinct, that was enough to secure a Cruz win. Had Ted Cruz not cheated, in all likelihood Dr. Carson would have retained those measly 4.15 votes per precinct thus giving the Iowa win to Donald Trump.

Whether Dr. Carson would've been able to snag those votes on his own merit is yours to decide but I think the numbers tell a clear enough picture. But time to move on.

Avatar: Brick Wilson suggests and I agree:
"Trump will win New Hampshire and the last remaining talking point will be refuted: "Will his supporters get out and vote?" Iowa was basically a 3 way tie, and Ted won one extra delegate. But, was it worth it? He (Cruz) cut off his nose to spite his face. Meanwhile Trump, who was never really expected to win Iowa because of the evangelicals, made a gallant attempt and came up just short. The more important point is that Trump, the anti-politician, the businessman, the scourge of the establishment, just got a handful of GOP delegates. The symbolism of that has a greater impact than you might at first imagine. You cruzbots have 5 days to crow. 5 days."

*A*vatar: *Isaac Abraham* posted this humorous comment inspired by the Cruz Campaigns misleading tweet about Dr. Carson:
Breaking News at CNN via Twitter.
Canadian PM Justin Trudeau just tweeted, banning Donald Trump from entering Canada, for insulting Ted Cruz citizenship and Canada.
Donald Trump's campaign just tweeted that Trump is leaving the campaign in New Hampshire to go back to NY, to shop for some clothes at Macy's.
Jimmy Carter, after endorsing Donald Trump, was promised to get the ambassadorship to Iran to negotiate the Iran nuclear deal, 52 hostages were held for 444 days in Iran under him, so he knows Iran.
Hillary Clinton tweeted, as president, the white house

will give every women coming to visit, a can of dress stain remover.

Chris Christie tweeted, if elected as president, everyone who voted for me, will get a free EZ-Pass for the Washington Bridge.

Jeb Bush tweeted, if you elect me as president, free drinks on the White House.

Dr. Ben Carson's team just tweeted, Carson will stop tweeting and start twerking.

Mike Huckabee just tweeted, after joining Trump at the fundraiser for the Vets, will now do a fundraiser for the Pets.

Fox News just tweeted, we will not be out-FOXed by Trump.

Megyn Kelly just tweeted, I sleep with my Trumpet. Crazy as it gets, more to come after the debate."

Avatar: Bill
"Ted Cruz is one of the biggest slime-balls in Washington, and that is saying a lot."

Avatar: oncefiredbrass:
"Cruz has no appeal in other states. He better whoop it up while he has the chance, because quite a few losses are coming. He may have hoodwinked Iowans over the 10 months he camped out there, but things come faster now and his slick lawyer talk won't work in a lot of the states coming up!"

Avatar: THE RED DRAGON
"Iowa hasn't picked a winner in 20 years. And they continued that trend tonight. Cruz is unelectable. What state does he win next? Cruz is so slimy. And the

Establishment has picked their gang of 8 anchor baby. Trump or we're all screwed".

Avatar: JKKnox:
"Cruz was born on foreign soil, held dual citizenship up until a few months ago, and is a first term senator with few if any real accomplishments...our country has had enough first term senator nubcakes. Iowa just continued its streak of picking the not-nominee.

In addition his voting "violation" flier, and now these caucus hi jinxs lend credence to what his other scumbag politician jerks have said about him being a bigger jerk. Now that is a hard bar to climb over, being a standout jerk in DC."

Avatar: Lady ThreeFiftyFive:
"We have been telling the Cruz sycophants that he is a slimy snake oil salesman, are they going to listen now? His dirty tricks are coming to light with his hidden Goldman Sachs loans, voting violation ploy, Carson dropping out lie, and blatant Trump smears on caucus eve no less. This man Ted Cruz is a lying weasel!"

A total of thirty delegates are awarded in Iowa's Republican race, a fraction of the amount necessary to clinch the nomination. The final Iowa delegate count is this:

Ted Cruz   8
Donald Trump   7
Marco Rubio   7

Ben Carson	3
Rand Paul	1
Jeb Bush	1

After last night's Iowa results, former Governor of Arkansas Mike Huckabee has left the 2016 presidential race. I've always thought highly of Governor Huckabee as he's a man of integrity with a strong moral character.

I hope he will continue to speak to the political process of this nation and keep working to make a difference for the future of America. Thanks Governor Huckabee!

: Cactus1029 wrote:
"Carson presented absolutely no threat to Cruz. I like Carson, but he won't win. Shame on you, Ted."

Avatar: XGOPeestate:
"Of all people for Ted to screw, Dr Carson! That is a disgrace! TRUMP 2016!"

Avatar: cookiebob explains it like this:
"I don't see this as about who won or lost, or Donald Trump, I see this as cheating a really good man out of the votes he earned. I see this as a revelation of Cruz's lack of character and raw ambition at the expense of honesty.
We have a government like that now, we don't need a dishonest Republican to follow up Obama."

Avatar: Sandra Opines to cookiebob:

"Trump won by defying the odds in Iowa. He is all good. Cruz LIED and sold his soul for ONE state. He committed several illegal voter crimes. He exploited Christianity, his children, his own Constitutional beliefs and much more...all to win ONE delegate in Iowa.

That is essentially just how low Cruz has gone to date. I can only imagine how much lower he can go."

Avatar: Cookiebob to Sandra Opines:
"I am not supporting Trump, I will vote for him if he wins, but I don't see him as a great person, either...but I was really disgusted with Cruz and his exploitation of Christianity. That speech last night did not belong in a political campaign and then to find out he cheated. No thank you. I guess the word is hypocrite. Cruz is a hypocrite. He tries to be holier than thou and then praises God while he is cheating?"

Avatar: Mercy Moor:
"Cruz Control Campaign [CCC] slithers out from under a rock to intimidate Iowans with false voter mailers & shoved Carson out with lies to steal his votes. The slimy, slithering snake coils in innocence... we're just trying to get out the vote; btw: thanks for the Carson votes...ooops.
Cruz slowly slithers back under the rock and it's on to the NH gig. Cruz tactics makes his supporters proud of the snake that he is but all can see he wins by deception. Stay tuned."

Avatar: kjb0010:

"Cruz cheated, so what. Let's move on. Cruz got 8 delegates, Trump 7. There are so many other races to come and Cruz isn't so popular in most of those. At this point, 1 point doesn't make an election won, and well, let's face it. It's a good thing Trump came in second, since the Republican candidate that Iowa has picked has not gone on to win the nomination in at least several election cycles.
Congratulation to Donald Trump for his second place win and Congratulations to Ted Cruz for coming in first, now we'll see you all in New Hampshire. Happy Trails, Trump 2016."

Avatar: Phillip Klein:
Trump, you are one of the most honest, up front, loyal, patriotic public figures I've seen in a long time! I'm glad you are challenging Cruz, we need to get to the bottom this. If this is an example of what you will do as President. I'm with you 100% Thank you! and God Bless!
#TrumpTrain #Trump2016 #MakeAmericaGreatAgain
Let it be known that 1,544 people agree with Phillip Klein.

ANALYZING IOWA

Donald Trump comes in second in the Iowa caucus, conceding the win to Senator Ted Cruz in a stunning concession speech.
I have to say, when I saw that Cruz won, I was a bit nervous about how our boisterous billionaire candidate was going to react. Make no mistake, I love Donald

Trump, but he does had the tendency to step over the line once in a while. I was afraid that this loss to Cruz might set him off since the media, as always, was in full-blown "taunt Trump" mode, hoping for a Trump tantrum.

They were making me mad with their constant reporting of Trump's "humiliating defeat". I figured if they were making me mad, they were making him mad too. So I was nervous that he might take their bait.

I am so proud to say, I couldn't have been more wrong. Mr. Trump delivered a strikingly humble press conference in which he sincerely congratulated Ted Cruz on his win.

"We finished second. And I want to tell you something: I'm honored. I'm really honored. And I want to congratulate Ted. And I want to congratulate all of the incredible candidates," Trump told supporters Monday night.

Donald Trump has maintained since day one, he only wants to be treated fairly. The Megyn Kelly debate fiasco was a perfect example of that. He wasn't treated fairly in that debate with her "War on Women" sham accusation and he fought back. We all fought back, but Kelly still has her job and reputation today even if it is slightly tarnished by her actions of late.

Some said Trump behaved like a petulant child in his war with Ms. Kelly. I say, he stood up for himself and I was so glad he did.

To be fair, Trump made a few mistakes on his way to Iowa and if the Ted Cruz lie really didn't affect the results all that much causing Donald Trump to lose fair and square, then below are ten possible reasons why that might have happened, according to Newsmax.com.

1. Trumps attack on Carson — "Trump lost Iowa largely for one reason: he crushed Ben Carson," Newsmax CEO Chris Ruddy wrote in a Tuesday column, noting that the famed neurosurgeon was once favored to win the state. "Trump used his verbal powers and eviscerated Carson. Carson's poll numbers collapsed, his campaign staff quit, and his fund-raising machine ground to a halt. But it was a Pyrrhic victory for Trump because the Carson voters didn't back him — they switched to Cruz!"

2. He gaffed about stupid Iowans — In the week leading up the caucus, Ted Cruz ran an ad that showed Donald Trump struggling to articulate himself, The Washington Post reported. "How stupid are the people of Iowa?" Trump is heard asking his followers at a rally. In context, Trump was asking the audience if they really believed a story about Ben Carson's troubled youth, but Cruz's TV spot did not provide that context, leaving viewers to wonder why Trump would ask such a question. Salon also noted that Trump re-tweeted a follower who asked "Too much Monsanto in the corn creates issues in the brain?" Those comments together didn't set well with Iowans.

3. He once supported abortion — *Keep the Promise*, the network of super PACs supporting Sen. Ted Cruz, ran an effective attack ad in the week before the caucus that showed Donald Trump's 1999 interview with the late Tim Russert, The Washington

Post reported. In the clip, Trump says he's "very pro-choice in every respect." He goes on to say he would not ban partial-birth abortion as president. While Trump has declared himself pro-life these days, his past comments likely hurt his campaign.

4. Evangelicals who made up 64 percent of the 2016 (Iowan) electorate abandoned him in droves. And that pretty much explains Cruz's victory," wrote The Weekly Standard. "He won 34 percent of evangelicals, while Trump won 22 percent and Rubio won 21 percent. Among the 36 percent of caucus-goers who aren't evangelicals, Trump took 29 percent, Rubio took 26 percent, and Cruz took 18 percent."

5. He skipped the Fox News debate which Fox contributor Charles Krauthammer said Monday night, that Trump's decision to skip the debate was "kind of a slap in the face" to Iowa voters and "allowed the others to come out and shine."

6. Some believe that the Sarah Palin endorsement actually hurt him. While some said Palin's endorsement of Trump would help him with evangelicals and Tea Partiers, many pundits wondered aloud if her endorsement would actually hurt the Trump campaign in the end. Many pundits still blame her for McCain's loss in 2008, and after Fox News decided not to renew her contract last year, *FiveThirtyEight* noted that "her net favorability rating among Republicans has declined more than 55 percentage points since 2008, from +83 percentage points to +27 points by mid-2013."

7. National Review attacked him just 10 days ahead of the Iowa caucus. The conservative magazine released a special issue, "Against Trump," in which more than 20 prominent conservatives, including Glenn Beck, William Kristol, and John Podhoretz, argued against nominating Trump.

8. He may have relied on polling too much? At campaign rallies, debates, and in the media, Donald Trump often touts a series of national polls, which are often conducted via land-line telephones, according to *Townhall*. "Ask yourself how many people do you know personally that have given up land-lines," the publication wrote.

9. "Trump created a large enough pool of people to win the Iowa caucuses but unfortunately his campaign was unable to convert them to voters," said Roger Stone, a one-time Trump adviser, according to Politico. The publication noted that Cruz had the superior get-out-the-vote infrastructure set up in Iowa, including a top-notch database to target potential voters with mailings and digital ads.

10. Trump didn't spend the money he needed to — Politico reported that "A source said the Trump campaign balked at the price tag associated with Cambridge Analytica's services," a best-in-class data firm. "Instead, Trump's data shop is headed by a pair of low-profile former RNC data engineers, Matt Braynard and Witold Chrabaszcz, who are regarded as technically savvy but who do not have previous high-

level campaign experience." Cruz's campaign spent at least $3.6 million on his data firm, while it appears Trump spent about $235,000 on his through the end of 2015, according to Politico.[161]

Has the Trump Campaign learned anything from this past week? Only time will tell.

On to New Hampshire. We will see you there.

THE ROAD TO NEW HAMPSHIRE

THE GOP IS CLUELESS, AS USUAL

While reading the surveys from Trump supporters and comments on-line, I began to see a recurring theme in the way people felt about the current Republican Party. The people are angry and they very much want to take that anger out on the Establishment class.

In the election of 2014, the people gave the Republican party a massive victory. It was a referendum on the destructive policies of President Barack Obama and the Republicans promised the voters that if we gave them power they would stop Obama in his tracks. They even promised to repeal Obamacare and various other unconstitutional actions taken by an out of control President. They said everything we wanted to hear and we trusted them at their word.

They betrayed us by turning a blind eye to the damage Obama was doing. They would give press conferences, assurances to us that they were doing everything they could to fight Obama but in the end, they did nothing. They caved on every bill the Obama Administration put forth, even funding Obamacare, Planned Parenthood and Obama's unconstitutional Executive Amnesty. They passed the Omnibus Bill, a budget that will devastate our country and our children's futures. They have given Obama everything he wanted while they ignored the will of the people.

They went so far as to tell us that we were too stupid to know what was best for us. Jonathan Gruber, Professor of Economics at the Massachusetts Institute of Technology, and a former technical consultant to the Obama Administration, worked with both the administration and U.S. Congress to help write the Patient Protection and Affordable Care Act (ACA), also known as Obamacare. Gruber was caught on video stating what he and the Obama Administration apparently thought about the American people.

Many of the videos show him confessing to the misleadingly ways in which the ACA was crafted and marketed. In order to get the bill passed, Gruber said the bill had to be written in a way as to disguise the facts and confuse the people.

Gruber said this obfuscation was necessary because of the "stupidity of the American voter", he stated the bill's inherent "lack of transparency was a huge political advantage" in selling it. In some of the videos he specifically refers to American voters as ill-informed or "stupid".

The Democrats rammed Obamacare down the throats of Americans but when the Republicans were given power of both chambers with the 2014 election, they did nothing to stop it, they even funded it.

The ACA creates a system by which "the young and healthy people pay huge premiums while sick people get the benefits". Premiums and deductibles have skyrocketed, even though we were promised they wouldn't, while the benefits are pretty much useless.

In order to get any benefit from Obamacare, you pretty much have to be hit by a bus. Had the people known the truth about it, the politicians would never have gotten it passed.

Currently Americans feel like there is no difference between the Republicans and the Democrats and judging from their actions, that may be true. The GOP have forgotten who they work for and where they came from and instead they have become cohorts with the Democrats and the Obama Administration.

They are bought and paid for by their lobbyist, and the ACA is a perfect example of that. Most of the country was opposed to the ACA but the politicians didn't listen as we screamed and protested. We have found out now that the plan was written by insurance companies, lobbyist and donors and nary a single representative took the time to read the bill before they passed it. The insurance companies took care of themselves by writing in a bailout clause, while the rest of us got screwed in the process as we lost our doctors and could no longer afford the Affordable Care Act (ACA).

They also ignored us on the debt, illegal immigration, securing our borders and protecting our nation. They didn't do a single thing we mandated of them and in doing so, they created the Trump Movement.

The GOP establishment considered Trump a joke right from the beginning. They never took him or his supporters seriously, considering the entire thing to be nothing more than a flash in the pan.

They have been in denial as poll after poll shows the unbelievable support that Mr. Trump receives and they haven't figured it out that the more they attack Mr. Trump, the more popular he becomes.

With the candidacy of Donald Trump and the possibility of his winning the White House, the current GOP have joined forces with the Democrats in their effort to stop a Trump win. They seem to think that if they just hit on the right Trump transgression, they will destroy his chances. They have thrown everything they can think of at him, and he is still standing tall. They can't figure out this movement that has overtaken their otherwise docile and complacent electorate.

One question I keep asking myself is this. Are the GOP elite really that ignorant of the Trump tsunami coming their way or are they nonchalant about Trump because the game is already rigged. Most people think the later, but I really hope they are wrong.

Byron York wrote an article called "GOP Fear and Loathing in New Hampshire" and in it he speaks to the ignorance of the GOP he came into contact with. While at the First-in-the-Nation Presidential Town Hall, at the Nashua Radisson, York witness a "remarkable level of confusion, frustration, and just plain bewilderment at what is going on…" within the party, on the faces of the local officials, activists, and politicos who attended the gathering. York asked them, "How is it that Donald Trump is leading his closest competitor by nearly 20 points? They are perplexed, claiming not to know "anybody who supports him."

After that York asked everyone he met, "Do you know anyone who supports Donald Trump?" In nearly all cases, their answer was no.

Given Trump's big lead in the polls, how is it that so many Republicans politicians don't know about the

Trump movement. Either the public polls are wrong or there is some serious denial going on within the GOP Establishment.

York found one exception while talking to two officials, one county and one regional. They agreed that they knew a lot of Trump supporters who were "inexplicably devoted to him — unfazed by Trump's lack of policy specifics or any of his controversial statements".

York stated that most of the politicos in Nashua didn't deny the polls, they just explained that they "haven't personally encountered evidence that the Trump-dominated polls are accurate".

"I don't see it." "I don't feel it." "I don't hear it." Athey say over and over again.

"So what explains the polls?" York asked.

"I don't know." Was their only reply.

The big worry among Republicans is that there is a Trump movement that they can't see.

While having dinner with former New Hampshire Gov. John Sununu and his wife Nancy, the presidential race came up. Sununu who knows about everyone politically reportedly said some version of "I don't know what is going on" about a dozen times, according to Byron York.

York asked Mr. and Mrs. Sununu whether they knew anyone who supports Trump when they looked at each other for a minute, thinking, and finally said "Yes, there's a guy down the street from them who does."

York spoke with one Republican political operative who does a lot of work in New Hampshire, describes "driving down a street on the west side of Manchester, checking out the houses and noticing Trump signs in front of houses that he knew had never displayed signs before."

Republican elected officials are in a delicate position when it comes to Trump. Most of them don't like him but they also know how popular he is with the voters. Those who are inclined to criticize Trump, stay quiet because they have seen that the more they criticize him, the more popular he becomes.

Instead, they stick their collective heads in the sand and pretend that the polls are inaccurate, that some malfunction has occurred and the numbers can't be true. They claim the samples are too small or the margins of error too large, or any excuse they can come up with because the alternative is unfathomable to them

"I don't understand it," another Republicans who doesn't know any Trump supporters told York, "It doesn't make logical sense."[162]

I would've loved to have been standing beside Byron while he talked to these politicians, if for no other reason than to see the stupefied looks on the faces of the Elite GOP.

The Republicans and Democrats alike can't get their heads around Donald Trump or his supporters. They never thought Donald Trump would make it this far and they are perplexed, with no idea of how to stop his momentum. There's no way they are going to let "The People's Choice" make it to the finish line because if they do, their little party is over. That is one thing they are certain about.

One articulate blogger feels the same way:

Avatar: RightLane1111 posted on February 12,2015

"This is where the Republican Party proves that they are the party of STUPID. There is only ONE CANDIDATE...just one that will bring states into play that the Republicans have not won in a long time. Trump can do that...Cruz cannot. Let's just take pro-choice out of the picture...When Cruz said Trump had New York values, he just dissed a state that, if elected, he is sworn to protect and SERVE. I am originally from New York, I am Christian, I am Conservative...but that was plain STUPID on Cruz' part. STUPID.

So whoever doesn't not ascribe to Cruz' line of thinking has bad values??? Excuse me...but I want to know about Cruz (or his wife's) association with this North American Union BS under Bush. In fact...I would like to know about his HB1 visas. What has HE passed in the Senate? IN ONE SENTENCE...AND THIS IS THE CLOSE TO THIS CRUZ DEAL...HOW IS TED CRUZ GOING TO UNITE ANYONE? Republicans...better save your hide and get with the candidate who can, because this is YOUR LAST CHANCE BEFORE YOUR PARTY GOES BYE BYE."

Thank you RightLane1111, you are absolutely right.

Avatar: maxedgar:
"What so many of the elites on both sides fail to realize is we are tired of them. Think many of the young people realize that these elites have done

nothing for this country. It's the opposite - they have caused untold damage to this country. They have a choice pick a group that causes the problems or pick an individual with a history of success. It's not a hard choice."

THE NEW HAMPSHIRE POLLING

Donald Trump maintains a strong lead in New Hampshire, earning 31% of the vote in the Presidential Republican Primary polls. Jeb Bush leads the field in the race for second place with 14%, followed by John Kasich at 12% and more distantly by Marco Rubio with 10%, Ted Cruz at 9% and Chris Christie eeks out a 6% share.

Trump's advantage increases among likely voters who identify with the Republican Party to 34% while Bush garners 16%. Trump leads John Kasich among likely independent primary voters with 23% to Kasich's 16%. Marco Rubio gets 12% of the independents while Bush attracts 11%.

Among Democrats who say they are likely to vote in the Republican primary, Donald Trump and Carly Fiorina tie with 20% each.

Although Trump leads in every region of the state, Jeb Bush increases his proportion of the vote substantially in the Boston area with 18% and with 21% in the Portland-Auburn area. Jeb Bush and Marco Rubio tie at 15% for second in the Burlington - Plattsburgh market and Kasich pulls into second in Hillsborough County with 18% and Rockingham

County with 11%. Trump has comparable leads among both women with 28% and men at 32%.

While Trump leads among the three older age brackets (40-54: 39%, 55-65: 31%, 66+: 26%), Jeb Bush shows strength among younger voters aged 18 to 39 with 25% to 26% for Trump. Among self-identified Very Conservative voters, Trump leads 32% followed by Ted Cruz at 18% and Jeb Bush with 16%. He also leads among Somewhat Conservatives at 35% followed by Jeb Bush at 14% and Rubio at 13%. John Kasich leads Trump among Moderates 25-24% while Bush attracts 14% of that group.

Note: Gilmore, Huckabee and Santorum each earned 0% of the vote.

When it comes to favorability among the candidates, only Donald Trump maintains a 51% favorable rating against a 47% unfavorable rating. This gives Donald Trump a net favorable image rating among likely Republican primary voters heading into in New Hampshire.

John Kasich and Jeb Bush both struggle with a 45% favorable to a 50% unfavorable, making them the only other candidates coming anywhere close to a 50% rating.

Trump's image advantage is even more obvious when we compare the Very Favorable ratings. A full 37% plurality of likely voters say they have a very favorable opinion of Donald Trump. This number falls to 18% and 15% for Kasich and Bush, respectively.[163]

This is the poll I've been waiting for, the first 7 News/UMass Lowell tracking poll of New Hampshire that includes reaction to the Iowa Caucus.

Donald Trump is still in first place, but he's frozen at 38%. Ted Cruz is second at 14%, while Marco Rubio comes in third with 12% of the likely votes. Jeb Bush has 9% and John Kasich has 7%.

Rounding out the remaining Republicans are Chris Christie with 6%; Ben Carson and Carly Fiorina with 3% each and Rand Paul with 2% while 6% of voters still remain undecided.

Here's what I see going into the New Hampshire primaries: Trump is on top, but not moving. Cruz stays in second while Rubio jumps up two points. Jeb Bush is holding steady while John Kasich is not receiving the reception he wanted. He's down two points.

On the Democrat side of the aisle, Bernie Sanders still looks like he'll win, but even though Clinton is cutting into his lead, she still has a mountain to climb. Sanders gets 61% in the poll to Clinton 32% while 5% of Democrats voters claim to still be undecided.

Tracking polls shows some slight Clinton momentum, she's up two points and Sanders is down two points, so for Hillary Clinton simply to come close in New Hampshire, could almost be as good as winning.[164]

By this time next week, we'll know the outcome of both races and a clearer picture will begin to surface.

THE WEEK BEFORE

LITTLE ROCK, ARKANSAS FEBRUARY 3, 2016

In 1974, the Barton Coliseum in Little Rock Arkansas had a record breaking show featuring ZZ-

Top that drew a stunning 11,107 people but tonight that record was broken. It wasn't another rock band, comedian or sporting event that broke the long-time record, it was something Little Rock had never seen before. It was inconceivable to some that something so mundane could draw such a massive crowd, but there it was.

On this day, Wednesday, February 3, 2016, Donald Trump beat ZZ-Top with 11,500 in attendance and more still arriving. The event is over an hour late but the excitement continues to grow with each passing minute.

Some people have been there since early this morning, hoping to be first in line while others will be turned away by Fire Marshals as they try to squeeze themselves into the overly crowded building.

When Secret Service finally appears, the crowd takes notice. They get their cell phones ready for videos and photos of their soon to be President, Donald Trump arrives to a packed house of adoring fans. As he takes the stage, the crowd goes wild and once again The American Love-Fest with Donald Trump is front and center for all to see.

Trump Rally in Little Rock, Arkansas on Feb, 3, 2016

EXETER, NEW HAMPSHIRE, FEBRUARY 4, 2016

Cars line the streets heading out of town, as hordes of supporters show up for Donald Trump's NH Rally at the Exeter Town Hall today, February 4, 2016.

The billionaire is drawing crowds like we've never seen before. At noon on a Thursday, you wouldn't expect to see lines like this, but for Donald Trump, this is the norm. Everywhere he goes, people stop what they are doing just to go see him speak. He's breaking attendance records all over yet there arc still many thousands of disappointed people turned away at nearly every rally, as Fire Marshalls stretch the limits, trying to accommodate everyone who wants to see our next President.

Today's rally is being held at the historic Exeter Town Hall and true to form, it's a love-fest.

CBS News reporter Jacqueline Alemany posted a photo to Twitter showing a long line of parked cars of rally attendees on a street that extended out of town.

Later she reported on the atmosphere outside the hall before Trump spoke with this Tweet:

"Steam rising, Stones blasting, signs being tossed into the mosh pit of a crowd – the energy for @realDonaldTrump in Exeter is infectious."

Another photo posted to Twitter by the Cook Report's Dave Wasserman shows Fox News Sunday host Chris Wallace and crew being blocked from entering the hall.

Wasserman tweets out to his followers:

"Mad scene in Exeter, NH for Trump. Fire Marshal just turned a perplexed Chris Wallace & @FoxNews away"

HMM. Now that's very interesting !!!

Exeter, New Hampshire Rally Feb. 4, 2016 by Getty Images, Andrew Burton

Donald Trump greets the crowds after the rally in Exeter, NH.

I wonder how many times Donald Trump has signed his name?

Donald Trump has held so many rallies across New Hampshire in the weeks before the Primary, and it was the same all over. No matter where he goes from Manchester to Salem, the crowds adore him. They believe in him and for the first time in a very long time, people actually have HOPE once again. Donald Trump "built that" and we the People, can't get enough of Donald Trump and the American Love-Fest.

A NOBEL NOMINATION FOR

DONALD TRUMP

Donald Trump, the GOP front-runner, has just accomplished another first for him. He's joined an exclusive group of about 200 individuals, which includes Greek Islanders helping desperate migrants; Angela Merkel, the Chancellor of Germany, Edward Snowden, and the Pope.

While some of these may seem more likely than others, all are understood to be in the running for the 2016 Nobel Peace Prize.

The Director of the Peace Research Institute of Oslo and Nobel Watcher Kristian Berg Harpviken confirmed the GOP front-runner has been nominated for the award.[165]

According to a copy of the nomination letter Harpviken claims to have received, the outspoken, multi-billionaire Trump has attracted international attention by calling for a ban on Muslims entering the

United States. The Nobel Committee claims that Donald Trump deserves the nomination for "his vigorous peace through strength ideology, used as a threat weapon of deterrence against radical Islam, ISIS, nuclear Iran and Communist China."

Trump's reported nomination comes after a number of inflammatory and divisive comments made in the run-up to the Iowa caucus. By proposing Muslims be temporarily banned from entering the US and his condemnation of our broken immigration system and wide open borders that allow illegal Mexican migrants to flood our country, he's certainly captured the attention of millions of Americans. They want our country protected and Trump's promise to build a "big beautiful wall" between the U.S. and Mexico has without a doubt garnered Mr. Trump the support of most of the country.

Donald Trump has a better chance of winning the Presidency than he does a Nobel Peace Prize but the honor of the nomination alone must make him feel extremely vindicated. The world gets his message, even if the Main Stream Media does not.

Avatar: 7PATTY_HENRY7:
"TRUMP SHOULD WIN this... HE is 1000% correct: PEACE THROUGH STRENGTH. I doubt that those liberals would ever give it to him, but He deserves it! Another thought, I have total confidence that TRUMP could get into a room with almost all our enemies and work out a lasting Peace (Islam, Iran not included because they do not want peace, they want world domination) but everyone else who has a beef

with USA or vice versa? I know he could!! GO TRUMP!!'"

THE REPUBLICAN DEBATE IN NEW HAMPSHIRE

ABC News' David Muir and Martha Raddatz will host the seventh Republican Debate from St. Anselm College in Manchester, N.H., airing tonight, Saturday, February 6, 2016.

A much smaller field of Republican presidential hopefuls will be on the stage in New Hampshire, but in the end, that didn't make for a cordial debate; in fact, many called it a outright "Blood-bath".

Donald Trump, Ted Cruz, Marco Rubio, Ben Carson, Chris Christie, Jeb Bush and John Kasich all took part in the ABC News debate, with just days until the New Hampshire primary.

The debate is the first since Ted Cruz pulled off his somewhat sleazy victory over Ben Carson, securing the Iowa win. It also marks the return of Donald Trump to the debate stage following his boycott of the previous GOP showdown on Fox News.

I think everyone, from the candidates and their staff to the Americans watching at home, are a bit sick of these debates. We don't generally learn anything new, we just watch to see if anyone implodes in front of our eyes. For some, especially certain moderators, it's a game of sport, as they do their best to take down a candidate as opposed to providing the American public an impartial forum in which to examine our options.

This debate was no different. It was a fiasco from the start.

The ABC debate began with a glitch as each of the candidates were being introduced. The first name called to the stage was Chris Christie. The applause lingered through the time when Martha Raddatz called the second candidate Ben Carson.

Not hearing his name called amidst the loud applause, Dr. Ben Carson missed his cue, causing a pretty uncomfortable traffic jam in the narrow tunnel leading to the podiums.

As awkward as it was to watch, Ben Carson was even more uncomfortable. He didn't know what to do, so he simply stood in the tunnel, on live TV yet out of sight of the moderators and the audience. Ted Cruz was called next and had no problem walking right passed the confused Neurosurgeon to take his place on-stage.

The fourth name called was Donald Trump, and as he entered the tunnel, he realized the embarrassing position his fellow candidate was in.

Some people say that Donald Trump didn't hear his name either, causing him as much confusion as poor Ben Carson. I saw it differently. I saw a man who understood the embarrassment that the Good Doctor was feeling and made a quick decision to stand with the fallen man instead of leaving him behind to suffer the humiliation alone. Donald Trump remained in the tunnel with his colleague, thereby reducing any anxiety being felt by Dr. Carson.

It would've been easy for Trump to walk on by, just like all the other candidates, but instead he chose to wait with Dr. Carson, showing tremendous leadership qualities, as well as empathy for another human being.

When Dr. Carson was finally called to the stage, Trump waited to allow the embarrassed doctor a chance to get the audience response and appreciation that he deserved.

It takes a lot of courage to make split second decisions like this, and it shows a remarkable insight into the man's character.

People often mistake Donald Trump's self-confidence for arrogance or even narcissism. But I don't know a single narcissist on the planet who would've put themselves in a position like that just to assist his competition.

Trump and Carson remained civil to each other all night while insults were flying between Chris Christie and Marco Rubio, while Ted Cruz was taking it from all sides. A particularly nasty exchange took place between Front-Runner Donald Trump and Governor Jeb Bush, who said he was "sick and tired" of the the real-estate mogul "going after my family".

"While Donald Trump was building a reality TV show, my brother was building a security apparatus to keep us safe," the former Florida governor said. "And I'm proud of what he did. And he (Trump) has had the gall to go after my brother."

Mr. Trump's response of "the World Trade Center came down during your brother's reign, remember that", was met with exaggerated boos from an over-zealous audience that didn't hesitate to inject their own sound effects into the already feisty proceedings.

I watched ABC's live stream and they had a few young reporters covering a focus group of students from a New Hampshire college (bribed with free pizza, of course) in an auditorium. During a cut to commercial, the reporter was told to ask the kids if any Trump supporters had lost faith in Trump due to his performance thus far. The Majority shouted that they were still supporting Trump.

As if that wasn't clear enough, the reporters asked the kids who they thought was winning the debate tonight.

As I heard the TRUMP! TRUMP! TRUMP! TRUMP! chant begin, the reporter said with his finger in his ear "It's not quite clear who exactly won because I can't hear over the noise." I shrugged my head in disgust because even over the loud noise, I could clearly hear what the young people of America thought about the debate. Maybe this reporter needs to have his hearing checked.

It seemed to me, and everyone else too, that Donald Trump won the debate in a stunning fashion by calling out the debate audience for being part of the political donor class. Yes, it's true, those dreaded donors filled the auditorium with their Anti-Trump boos and Pro-Bush cheers.

It was a jaw-dropping moment in political history for a candidate to openly call out the hypocrisy of the party in a live forum such as this but Donald Trump breaks all the rules and lets the chips fall where they may.

A few days later when it came out that Trump was right and most of the seats did go to donors, lobbyist and special interest groups and not to the general public at large, the People clearly saw it for what it was and it angered them even more. But the upside to it all was that it showed just how brave Donald Trump really is and what power his words carry because after he called out the audience, they began to moderate their own behavior. It was stunningly obvious that Donald Trump had put this audience in their place. A true leader.

Incredible debate, absolutely incredible.

Avatar: Falcon:
"ROFL!! Bush attacking Trump is like a Chihuahua attacking a Pit Bull - the Pit Bull will mostly ignore it ..... until he gets tired of the endless noise - then with one bite, the Chihuahua's gone. [One on one, Bush doesn't stand a chance - Trump will eat him alive]."

Avatar: True American!:
"As a TRUMP supporter this is why I support him!! Now that said he needs to let the BUSH thing go, you did your damage, now move on TRUMP, let's talk about the real issue MUSLIMS!!-- and the threat they cause!! I understand there's a better chance at winning the Power-ball than Trump reading this post but my god let the BUSH thing go!! just keep hammering what every real American knows, that the Muslims pose a threat here and abroad!"

Avatar: Preacher:
'Jeb thinks he can swap punches with a seasoned street-fighter like Donald Trump -- NOT GOOD!"

THE PEOPLE ARE ECSTATIC

Donald Trump crushes the competition to win the New Hampshire Primary in a landslide victory. He more than doubled that of the second place winner, Ohio Governor John Kasich, winning 35 percent of the vote to Kasich's 16 percent.

Senator Ted Cruz came in third place with 12 percent of the vote essentially deflating his dubious win in Iowa last week. Former Governor Jeb Bush came in fourth, followed by Senator Marco Rubio, Governor Chris Christie, Former CEO Carly Fiorina, Dr. Ben Carson, Senator Rand Paul, former Governor Mike Huckabee and former Senator Rick Santorum, the last two receiving zero votes each.

Sean Hannity and Donald Trump discuss the obtuse GOP elite and their loss to Donald Trump on The Hannity Show on Feb 11, 2015. Hannity talks about two headlines he's been reading, the Byron York piece and one where the GOP asks "Can Trump and Cruz Be Stopped?" Hannity is as perplexed as the rest of us for the GOP's denial of who their front-runner is. Hannity asks Trump, "What part of this is the Republican establishment not understanding. That you won New Hampshire by a landslide and what part are they struggling with that you in N.H., Cruz in Iowa are the two insurgency guys they hate the most and you are winning. What part of that don't they get? Why don't they understand this?"

Trump believes that he would've won Iowa if Carson hadn't been treated so badly by what happened with Cruz. "The fact is that they're not in love with me because I'm not accepting their money and I can't be bought. I'm not gonna be bought. I'm a self-funder, they don't like self-funders."

Who cares if the establishment doesn't like the self-funder Donald Trump because that's one of the main things the American people do like about him. We demand someone who can't be bought. We want someone who will fight for us, not the special interest groups and donors. We are sick of our elections being stolen from us and we are sick of electing lying, self-serving politicians, who screw us every time in favor of their donors. We are sick of the elite politicians thinking that we're too stupid to notice what they are doing. We notice and we demand better.

The American People are extremely happy tonight with Donald Trump's performance in New Hampshire. These are some of their words:

Avatar: Diversity Soldier is excited, just like the rest of us:
"Trump killed it, I've never been so excited to vote in my life. I hope the upsets continue and then maybe Capitol Hill will WTFU!! The people are speaking. Trump2016"

Avatar: Oinia quotes Stephen Hayes:
"Donald Trump won every issue, and he won every issue decisively." Hayes.
Trumpmentum growing. Eradicate the Establishment."

Avatar: Spartacus300 talks Cruz and dirty tricks:
"This was a great state to demonstrate who can draw voters of all makes and models!
Tebow Ted beat Trump by 4% in Iowa after all of his dirty tricks. With his lies and dirty tricks he barely stole Iowa. Now Trump stole the show! And by a very decisive 24%. Cruz got B slapped back to where he belongs. Filthy donor slave insider political scum! TRUMP FOR VICTORY!!!!!"

Avatar: Dixie comments on Kasich's chances going forward:
"When Kasich heads to S.C., if he even bothers to, he will instantly become a non-starter. Kasich will never gain traction anywhere in Dixie. He has served nicely as a wedge between strongman Trump and a weak secondary field of contenders in the N.H. primary. But, that is as far as he is going to get before he, too, drops out.
Can Trump win primaries? Hell, yes. I think he could sweep every state through the SEC Super Tuesday on 03/01/16. After that Trump will have so much momentum and so many committed delegates that he will become completely unstoppable. Refill your Valium prescription, Megyn Kelly. You're really going to need it now."

Avatar: Rachel Francon speaks openly:
"Hurrah Trump!!! Why? I am a Transgender Woman.
And I support him with all my heart. Both of them....
before and after....lol

It is time someone had the guts to raise the hulkster finger in support of this message...from all the way to JFK (with a twist for the times):
Ask not what the country can do for your "group" but what your "group" can do for the country".

All the other candidates are really Establishment; whatever, they might be, because they are dependent on what the established use of media to foment narrow-minded self concern over the interests of the Nation:

Nothing but fear driven exploitation to cobble together specific interest groups ie: gender/sex/race/age to seek to get the overburdened country to help their particular interest...as specific and not universal as it might be.

It is time to set aside our own preoccupation with our own slice of life. We are doing fine by all standards. And, yes, we all have a long way to go as the society becomes more and more well structured in its mosaic pattern.

That is a selfishness we must overcome.

And with a leader such as Mr. Trump to carry our torch, we shall be able to relax and to energize; to overcome it.

Billy Jack is quite pragmatic:

Without Trump, America's most important issue of the our generation, illegal immigration, wouldn't even be a part of the discussion. Same with stopping the influx of so-called refugees. Despite his flaws, he's my choice. Trump 2016 and 2020!"

Avatar: maga1 states:

"Donald Trump is the hope of America, he is not perfect but he is getting better every day. He is a producer; most politicians, Jeb, Cruz, Rubio, never created anything. Trump is sincere, he makes honest mistakes. We have to forgive him and give him room to grow, he is learning this dirty politics as he creates this movement.

I can see great things are happening. Trump is a producer, not a taker. He will run this country using the principles of sowing and reaping. No free lunch, that's how America became great. If a farmer doesn't sow seeds, he shouldn't be expecting any harvest.

Hard working Americans, now you have somebody who understands hard work and will go to D.C. to do the work for you.
America will be Great again. Thank You!"

Avatar: Vulgarian gives us a run-down:
"New Hampshire: Trump 100,000 votes and 10 Delegates.
Now heads into South Carolina where he has sustained a 36.7% avg and has a +19. And had crowds larger than any others. Be the same result as N.H.

Then off to Nevada where Trump has sustained a 37% and has a +21 and has the Hispanic at 25% which should give him the same result as N.H. and that will take out the rest of these posers."

Avatar: KDN believes this:
"This is what people like about Trump. He is not polished or politically correct. He speaks that you have no problem understanding him. He does not talk from a speech and he does not take donations from big

money or special interest groups. He also is able to get more bang for his buck. Look where Trump finished in N.H. compared to Bush who spent over 30 million."

Avatar: old printer man sums it up perfectly:
"America needs TRUMP FOR PRESIDENT 2016...We don't need another socialist, communist ruler for 8 more years! "GOD BLESS AMERICA". "THANK THE LORD FOR TRUMP"
Now it is on to South Carolina, where the winner takes all."

MORE WORDS OF WISDOM

Millions of Americans are sickened by too many years of incompetent, corrupt and self-serving politicians, who along with their complicit media has allowed this nation's standing in the world to be reduced to a shadow of its former self. Donald Trump has become the primary vehicle of their frustration.

The 2016 Presidential Election may very well prove to be the year of the I'VE HAD ENOUGH voter. They want their country back, and they appear to believe Donald Trump is sincere in his sharing of their desire to see America restored.

Below are some of their words, spoken from their hearts. And even though this is just a sampling, it is indicative of the mood of millions.

Avatar: Mi Too has a conversation with Jill:
"I'm finding it harder and harder to align myself with establishment Republicans that scorn Trump.......

Anyone that puts the party over the country is not interested in what's best for the country."

Avatar: Jill to Mi Too:
"Same here... and it's embarrassing considering all the Democrats that Trump is winning over."

Avatar: Mi Too back to Jill:
"That is exactly what it takes to win an election, reach voters on both sides..." END OF THREAD.

Avatar: CB:
"This Floridian and my entire family and everyone in my office is voting Trump."

Avatar: Constitution Reader:
Here are some stances Trump is taking on in the campaign:
1. Secure the border.
2. Protect Christians from discrimination/persecution.
3. Lower taxes.
4. Stop out of control spending.
5. Keep terrorists out.
6. Eliminate Common Core.
7. Strengthen our military.
8. Support our veterans.
9. De-fund Planned Parenthood.
10. Bring jobs back to America.
These are CONSERVATIVE principles."
Avatar: FIGARO:
"America is sick of politicians with empty promises."

"America needs a man with guts who says how it is."

"America will vote for Trump who is not a politician."

Avatar: Ilovemycountry:

"Trump said he's going to make Apple produce its products in the U.S. - does that sound like an empty promise to you? He also said he's going to make Mexico pay for the southern border wall - to me that sounds like an empty promise, what do you think? Oh, and he'll ban all Muslims from entering the U.S. - do you buy that?"

Avatar: Hammer&anvil:

"Trump is a man of his word and he will build the wall."

Avatar: lyoverland:

"Trump is consistently getting crowds in excess of 10,000 people. I'd say that gives the polls that put him well ahead some credibility. Anything can happen in the next two weeks (people can be fickle), but the overwhelming odds are in Trump's favor. I see no path for Rand Paul to win anywhere."

Avatar: Eyesonyou:

"Ron Paul: Trump 'Likely' to Be Nominee"

"It's about time the GOP started backing the people's choice and start acting like they care where this Country is headed. The Dems are going to be pulling every sham they can to put their gangster candidate in Office. Trump is the people's choice and

the GOP had better start paying attention, because if
the Liberals get the White House, this Country will be
no more."

Avatar: ken: Started this thread:
"If Trump does well in the first few primaries as
the polls indicate, then add all the positive media
coverage, and the huge crowds he draws at his rallies.
It is safe to say this election will be compared to 2008
with the only difference is the party and candidate."

Avatar: thoughtsonthat replied back to ken:
"Trump will never get the Leftist Media to give
him positive media coverage. They work for
Progressives. He has succeeded in spite of their huge
negative influence."

Avatar: SteveL entered and said this to
thoughtsonthat:
"He may be the very progressive they are hoping
for, knowing that the GOP is set to have an advantage
in this election and fearing that Hillary will self
destruct."

Avatar: thoughtsonthat, ended the thread with this
for SteveL:
"I considered that early on, and anything is
possible. But I've since determined that Trump is
sincere, and that he has good reason (and self-interest)
to bring back and defend the freedoms and opportunity
that Constitutional America afforded him."

Avatar: old printer man:

"Impossible to please the people all the time! TRUMP is God Sent to me! Trump is a good man and loves his country! America must become the "LIGHT OF THE WORLD"...We've always opened our doors to help those in need! America like other countries has a constitution which our current regime has ignored...We believe Trump will restore our constitution! I will vote for TRUMP 2016!"

Avatar: American Worker's Warrior:
"The RINOs are trying to use their definition of Conservative to dissuade Conservatives from voting for Trump. Just look at what these scumbags have helped do to this country for the last 25 years. These frauds have destroyed the meaning of Conservatism. Vote Trump and watch establishment septic tanks implode."

Avatar: willietasby speaks to the media:
"Hey National Review, Paul Ryan, Megyn Kelly, Nikki Haley, and all you GOPe, it's over, Trump will run the table. You and your ilk can run and hide. You are dead to us!"

Avatar: Dave C believes "Anti-Trump=Anti-American!"

Avatar: Cicero's Son:
"I love how Trump-who has done nothing but create jobs-is the "true conservative's" worst nightmare, while Paul Ryan-who has done nothing but destroy jobs and America-is viewed favorably. Conservatism is becoming a cult."

Avatar: Backdoor Barry:
"Watching the establishment lose their minds makes me giddy. And all this great entertainment is free, can you believe it?"

Avatar: OncealwaysaMarine:
"No GOP candidate, before Trump, has been able to survive the Democrat Super PAC MSM in recent presidential elections. They would eat Ted Cruz alive. No way he would win in the General because the MSM would destroy him. Donald Trump is the only GOP candidate since Reagan who has demonstrated any ability to snooker and turn the MSM narrative in any direction he wants. He single-handedly nipped Hillary's and the DNC's "war on women" faux issue in the bud! Who else would have done that? Cruz? I think not.

Trump ABORTED Bill Clinton's interjection into the race to help Hillary before he could make his first appearance at a Hillary campaign rally! You think Cruz could have done that?

Not only that, Trump has forced every other candidate (Democrat and Republican) to follow his lead and give an answer EVERY issue the cowardly RNC and armchair Media "conservatives" have been convincing GOP candidates for YEARS were taboo. They never would have been brought up if it weren't for Trump, let alone addressed with any seriousness.

No doubt in my mind who is the most electable candidate in this race. I'm not voting for a Conservative Philosopher; I'm voting for a President."

Avatar: Nunyour Bidnesky replied to
OncealwaysaMarine:
"Correct, the Establishment needs to be completely
purged from the GOP. It's time something gets done
about illegals, Muslim immigration, Muslim refugees,
and build the F'n wall. WE DON'T WANT TO
BECOME EUROPE! We don't want Americans
getting killed on American soil by idiot Jihadis."

Avatar: Mark E:
"These 22 are NOT conservative leaders. They're
conservative LOSERS. TRUMP is the only one
fearlessly leading the way and winning against the
political correctness that is not only destroying our
own nation, but also many other nations around the
world. GO DONALD TRUMP."

Avatar: rfred'sghost replies to Mark E:
"Bunch of Metros, not a backbone amongst them."

Avatar: Mark E back to rfred'sghost:
"Liberals thought they had this election in the bag
before Donald TRUMP turned their world upside
down. These so called "conservatives" were getting
little to no traction with the voters. Donald TRUMP
has changed all of that for the GOP. Now we've got
someone we can rally behind. TRUMP is a leader and
many many conservative and moderates agree totally
with pretty much everything the Donald is saying."

Avatar: Cvalert:
"YA GOTTA LOVE THE DONALD!! Wherever
he goes he keeps upsetting the "apple cart"...and he

does it everywhere he goes!!!!Go Donald!!! All the way to the White House!!!!!!!"

Avatar: Aksarben:
"That's the problem with trying to force your views on others. People want something done. They want elected officials to do the will of the people. Democrats never do the will of the people and now Republicans are now doing the same. The National Review comes out against Trump. Trump has promised to do the will of the people. And then The National Review says he's not Conservative enough. The Electorate would elect Joseph Stalin if they were assured he would do the will of the people. Everyone has forgotten the principles of a democracy!!!"

Avatar: Nashdroid:
"Has everyone seen the recent Reuters rolling poll nationally for the nomination?
REUTERS ROLLING: TRUMP 40.6%, CRUZ 10.5%, CARSON 9.7%, BUSH 9.2%
Holy crap! It's over!"

Avatar: Billy Beefcaked:
"Trump-ets unite! May the death of the Republic come quick under President Trump, and may the rise of the new Empire come forth!   Trump 2016!"

Avatar: Nunyour Bidnesky:
"I like 'giddy'. I guess that's how I am about Trump stomping their heads."

Avatar: colby anwar:

"Glenn Beck's poison touch killed his career last week and he's spending this week killing off Ted Cruz's. It's really, really, really, embarrassing for both of them. It's also even a little embarrassing for me to watch."

Avatar: Rob:
"The only thing missing from the Ted Cruz campaign is a stop in Louisiana, where he pulls two rattlesnakes out of a box, raises them above his head, and says, "Can I get a hallelujah?"

Cruz is going to have difficulty fending off a primary challenger in Texas at this point, much less beating Trump. Trump is not perfect, but Trump is a patriot. I do not question or doubt who President Trump will be working for in the White House: ME AND MY FRIENDS AND MY FAMILY! As for Glenn Beck, his ratings are falling, his emotional health is deterioration, and soon he'll be interrupting Bingo at the Shady Grove Retirement Center with a prediction of doom for the elderly people. I'm a Christian, but I have a creepy discernment issue with Cruz. Does he have real Faith, or is he trying to play us? Not my place to decide that though."

Avatar: Will Jones:
"Ever ask yourself why both parties and the media are anti-Trump? The only answer I can come up with is they don't want anyone to actually represent the American people. Everyone wants their own interests represented, whether it's the government, big business, gays, or illegals. If everyone in the media and gov are

fighting for the American people then why do the citizens keep losing?"

Avatar: Vulgarian:
"If current trends continue, Donald Trump is likely to achieve the historically very rare primary race hat-trick of Iowa, New Hampshire, and South Carolina which would put him in a prime position to then dominate the all-important Super Tuesday primary vote to be held on March 1st which has no fewer than fifteen states at stake."

Avatar: buzzbuck:
"History shows sometimes people say things and it sounds much different than what was meant. Patton got more headlines for things he said than Madonna. That does not mean that Patton was not a great general. Despite slapping a private and everything else Eisenhower picked Patton to lead the 3rd army and he kicked butt all the way to Berlin. Trump may be brash and not your conventional statesman, but he will make a great president, balance the budget, and make America great again. We all will see that he will calm down once the campaigning is over and it's time to sit down and take care of the business of making congress work for the people."

Avatar: guppy1957 wants to know:
"WHY IS TRUMP ALWAYS THE FIRST ONE TO ANSWER AMERICA'S PROBLEMS" FIRST WITH OUR VETS AND MILITARY PERSONNEL PROBLEMS.
FIRST TO STOP OPEN BORDERS.

FIRST TO STOP OPEN IMMIGRATION.
FIRST TO STOP TERRORIST MUSLIM
IMMIGRATION.
FIRST TO STOP CORRUPT ECONOMIC
DEALS THAT HURT AMERICANS.
FIRST TO STOP GUN CONTROL.
FIRST TO PROTECT FREEDOM OF SPEECH.
FIRST TO RESPOND WITH THE ANSWERS
REAL AMERICANS PRAY TO KNOW.
WHY IS HE ALWAYS FIRST? BECAUSE HE
DOES NOT NEED PERMISSION FROM ANYONE
TO DO WHAT IS RIGHT FOR ALL AMERICANS.
THE OTHERS NEED PERMISSION BECAUSE
THEY SOLD YOU OUT. NOT BOUGHT AND
PAID FOR BY SPECIAL INTERESTS
TRUMP IN THE TRENCHES FIGHTING FOR
YOU AND YOUR FAMILY
TRUMP 2016 +++++"

Avatar: Vulgarian: Speaks to Trump and the
Hispanic Voter:
"Trump is doing O.K. among Hispanics, far better
than media is selling, with 30% supporting and 19%
undecided; a generally fair expectation could get him
to an outstanding 40%. (Romney got around 30%;
G.W. Bush got around 40%)".

Hillary Clinton is dominating among the high
school education or less group while Trump wins the
4-year college and above crowd.

Donald Trump has a big lead among "political
junkies" while Clinton does better with lower
information voters.

So that puts this insufferable GOPe talking point to rest.

Now let's get down to why they need to sell it.

This is why those who want Marco Rubio, Jeb Bush or Hillary Clinton, will do anything to insure Donald Trump is defeated and removed. They would rather lose to Hillary , and yes they will vote for her if needed, and still hold power, than see Trump win and know their influence disappears with his arrival."

Avatar: American Born ????:

"Americans want Trump as their Negotiator-in-Chief. Because Donald Trump's message to a humiliated media establishment and the who's who list of has-beens and lick-spittles desperately struggling to shore-up the likes of Jeb Bush, John Kasich and Marco Rubio couldn't be clearer.

Trump reminds one a bit of Oliver Cromwell admonishing England's Rump Parliament in 1653 with these words: "You have sat too long here for any good you have been doing. Depart, I say, and let us have done with you. In the name of God, go."" TRUMP 2016 - 2025"

Avatar: buzman:

"Trump has balls the size of church bells...TRUMP TRUMP TRUMP !!!"

Avatar: MidAmerica2:

"We have gotten ourselves a General Patton."

Avatar: Tim says:

"DONALD TRUMP IS NOTHING SHORT OF AWESOME!

DONALD TRUMP FOR PRESIDENT ASAP!!

-TO CREATE JOBS AND GET BACK JOBS FROM MANY COUNTRIES.

-TO PUT IN PLACE HIS TAX PLAN THAT WILL REDUCE TAX FOR ALL AMERICANS AND, AT THE SAME TIME, CUT MANY SQUANDERING CREATED BY THE INCOMPETENT OBAMA AND HIS MINIONS.

-TO CREATE A COUNTRY WITH BORDERS AS OPPOSED TO LETTING ANYONE IN.

-TO CREATE PLANTS IN THE USA AS OPPOSED TO CREATING THEM IN CHINA, MEXICO, AND COMPANY!!

-TO IMPLEMENT SEVERAL MEASURES TO PREVENT ACTS OF RADICAL ISLAMIC TERRORISM ON US SOIL TO KEEP US SAFE AND TO GIVE US REAL SECURITY!!

-AND MANY MORE.

THE UTTERLY INCOMPETENT OBAMA HAS BANKRUPTED THE US BY INCREASING THE US NATIONAL DEBT FROM $10 TRILLION WHEN HE FIRST BECAME PRESIDENT TO NOW $19 TRILLION AND WHEN HE LEAVES OFFICE TO $21 TRILLION!!!

INCOMPETENT OBAMA IS A CURSE FOR THE USA AND THE SOONER HE LEAVES WITH HIS DEMOCRAT MINIONS, THE BETTER OFF THE US WILL BE!!!

HILLARY CLINTON'S PLAN AS A PRESIDENT? ADD AT LEAST MORE THAN $10 TRILLION ON TOP OF THIS ALREADY

ASTRONOMICAL $21 TRILLION THAT OBAMA WILL GIVE AMERICANS AS U.S. NATIONAL DEBT AT THE END OF HIS PRESIDENCY!!!

DO YOU THINK THE U.S. COULD TAKE THIS AMOUNT OF ABUSE, SQUANDERING AND INCOMPETENCE FURTHER ONCE MORE WITH HILLARY CLINTON AND STILL BE OK?!!!? NOT IN A MILLION YEARS!!!

AGAIN, REMEMBER TO BE REGISTERED FOR THE CAUCUS AND GO AND VOTE FOR DONALD TRUMP, AS HE WILL NOT WIN WITHOUT EVERY SINGLE VOTE THAT HE SHOULD GET."

Avatar: JM40:
"Trump is Gulliver striding in the land of the Lilliputians. Occasionally some of the nasty little trolls think they can bring him down. A giant fist corrects them. We see the burning embers of National Review and Fox News Channel."

Avatar: Wax:
"Trump is the only hope to save this country from these ravaging monsters from other countries like this pr**k Murdock and his best buddy Soros."

Avatar: aquaviva:
"I started this process as anti-Trump. His enemies have driven me into the warm embrace of The Donald."

Avatar: Girlie58:

"Trump is Trump! You either love him, or hate him. That is the beauty of the 2016 election. We have unconventional candidates in Trump, Cruz, and even Rubio, running for the highest seat in the office, that of the president. These candidates are just like us, we the people, in their manner of thinking. Trump is our voice, and one who could actually repair damage done to our country with jobs, jobs, and more jobs! I would also feel more secure with Trump as president! He is not perfect, but who is? But He is authentic!"

About Donald Trump:
"I've met a lot of people in life and I have found it best to form opinions about them by actually meeting them in person. In 2009 I agreed to do that TV show Celebrity Apprentice on NBC. This meant I had to move to NYC for 6 weeks and spend every day with Donald Trump, Ivanka Trump, and Don Jr. I really had no expectations. I think I was actually the only "Celebrity" that had a semi normal manual labor job. I think this gave me a very different perspective on things. I actually think Donald Trump had no idea who I was or what I actually did for a living. Over the next month I was able to observe him and his kids in their day to day routine. What I saw was a person that treated everyone with respect. Even the (Hispanic) guys in the mail room. He had coffee from the coffee machine and BS'd with them every single morning. Trash men and cops would stop him on the street and he would stop whatever he was doing and spend a little bit of time with every one of them. As the month went on I used my work hard work and perseverance to gain respect of the Trumps and most everyone around me.

I made it all the way to the top 3 and when I was let go Donald Trump stood up and shook my hand and said " Great Job Jesse".

Now I know that a lot of you will think that is some dumb reality TV show, not real life...and especially Not the presidency. Trust me I know that is very true, but the majority of the Anti-Trumps are basing their opinion of him on sound bites from that very same Reality TV Show. I think you should look above what the TV Network put out there to boost ratings. Nobody wants to watch somebody be a nice guy, they want to see him say "Your FIRED!". What I personally observed is a man that is perfectly suited to run this country. He is respectful to the little guy (which shows he worked hard to get where he is) and he is also tough as nails when he needs to be. The people he will appoint to key top positions will be top shelf, and you can bank if they don't perform? They will get the boot. Lastly the best quality I observed about Donald Trump is being a dad. This is by far his strongest quality. Ivanka is a super smart, driven woman. She shakes your hand firm and looks you in the eye when she talks to you. Donald Jr. Also has the same smarts and drive, but is also a pretty regular guy that has a "almost" restored '69 Camaro and loves to long range shoot (don't let anyone know I told you that). The poise in these two shows a lot in their parents. I think we are lucky to have his kids as part of the deal.

So before you guys react to what I have written here. One thing you know about me is good or bad I will always tell it like it is. This guy is the real deal, and will Make America Great Again. Thanks for reading.

Jesse James #jessejames

Avatar: CrystalClear:
"Americans are looking for the person best suited to:

1. Protect and defend our borders and national sovereignty.

2. Stop and deport those crossing our borders illegally.

3. Prevent the mass influx of medieval and incompatible valued Middle-Eastern Muslims.

4. Bust up the unholy alliance between corporate and foreign-interest lobbyists being represented by career politicians for their personal campaign financing, and

5. Who has the business experience and guts to make it clear to corporations that they have a responsibility to employ the Americans they want to buy their products.

These are all issues Donald Trump brought to the forefront. He is the only candidate who is actually committed to making these things happen. He is the only GOP candidate since Reagan who has demonstrated any ability to snooker and turn the MSM narrative in any direction he wants. Not only that, he has forced every other candidate (Democrat and Republican) to follow his lead and give an answer to these issues. They never would have been brought up if it weren't for Trump, let alone addressed with any seriousness.

If you see such a man being the next President of the United States as "an embarrassment," you don't need God to help you; you need a shrink.

All these other issues don't mean crap if we allow our country to be taken over by illegals and Islamists. Philosophizing on what is "liberal" and what is "conservative" hasn't fixed a single damned problem in this country. The man best suited to be the next president is not the one who thinks they need to take care of the poor, but who will fight to keep government out of the way of the poor learning that they have a responsibility to take care of themselves."

Avatar: Weezy79: gets the final word:
"Hey Cruzbots...Trump leads in N.C., S.C., GA., KY., TN., FL., MS., AL., AR. by 20 points and leads Teddy by 5 in Texas. Let's go further, Trump leads Cruz by 20+ in OH., MI., PA., and every N.E. state.
Wanna get into mountain and S.W. state polling? It's the same result, Trump dominates."

LOVE-FEST OR PASSING FANCY?

The back-biting going on right now between Trump and Ted Cruz is beginning to take its toll, not only on the candidates but the electorate as well.
If Mr. Trump isn't careful, the Love-fest American's have with him could easily become a passing fancy.
Unfortunately, I'm beginning to see slight disillusionment for some. Let's hope it doesn't continue.
I have a friend on Facebook, a good man and a loyal Trump supporter but one of those currently

disillusioned with his hero. In a moment of despair, he posted this to his Facebook page:

MY OPINION, FOR WHAT IT'S WORTH:
"Both Donald Trump and Ted Cruz are showing their immaturity by falling into the Republican establishment trap. I hope I'm wrong, but more and more I see the handwriting on the wall.
DIVIDE AND CONQUER:
Trump and Cruz are diminishing each other and turning off voters. The elected establishment has now formed up behind Marco Rubio, the Amnesty candidate. Rubio is seen as the mature person to lead the party because he stays out of the gutter and focuses on his main set of issues.

The "angry" electorate can turn on Trump and Cruz just as fast as they gravitated to them both over the past 7 months. The voters are very stupid, generally speaking.
REMEDY:
Trump needs to grow up and refrain from infantile tantrums, no matter what the issue. He needs to remember what got him the lead in the first place. Creating the top issues and sticking to them. If he fails to campaign on his positive outlook for America and continues to sink into the abyss of petty squabbles with Cruz, they both will fail in the end.
END GAME:
I'll be watching for the next month until after Super Tuesday. I hope somebody gets through to Mr. Trump. I'd hate to see him waste all his time and mine, too. His Mount Olympus sized ego neutralizes his battle against

political correctness. Trump is politically correct due to his own ego. That has to be cured and cured fast!"

I've spoken to him since this post and he's firmly on the Trump Train, however, his concerns are valid and shared by many. I speak to people from all over the country and most of them could find some negative characteristic about Donald Trump if they really wanted to, but for most people, they see the bigger picture and they know, that, yes, Donald Trump does have some traits they don't like but so what. His imperfections make him human and even though the media would like to bury him for them, they only instill trust for the People who support him because it proves that Donald J. Trump is just one of them. Warts and all.

I think it's safe to assume that the American Love-Fest with Donald Trump is here to stay.

Endnotes

[1] http://www.breitbart.com/video/2015/06/16/watch-ivanka-intros-father-donald-trump-presidential-announcement/

[2] https://en.wikipedia.org/wiki/The_Kew-Forest_School

[3] Bender, Marylin (August 7, 1983). "The empire and ego of Donald Trump". The New York Times. .

[4] Solotaroff, Paul (September 9, 2015). "Trump Seriously: On the Trail With the GOP's Tough Guy". Rolling Stone.

[5] Barbaro, Michael (September 8, 2015). "Donald Trump Likens His Schooling to Military Service in Book". The New York Times.

[6] Strauss, Valerie (17 July 2015). "Yes, Donald Trump really went to an Ivy League school". The Washington Post.

[7] Max Ehrenfreund (July 22, 2015). "A secret to Donald Trump's success that you simply can't replicate". The Washington Post.

[8] Trump: the art of the deal, Paperback, ISBN 978-0-446-35325-0

[9] https://en.wikipedia.org/wiki/Donald_Trump

[10] http://www.people.com/article/donald-trump-brother-fred-death-alcoholism

[11] http://www.people.com/article/donald-trump-brother-fred-death-alcoholism

[12] http://www.phillymag.com/news/2015/08/16/donald-trump-atlantic-city-empire/

[13] Rozhon, Tracy (June 26, 1999)."Fred C. Trump, Postwar Master Builder of Housing for Middle Class, Dies at 93".The New York Times.

[14] http://www.businessinsider.com/donald-trump-net-worth-2015-7

[15] "Barbara Walters Is Shocked that Melania Trump Is Smart Because She's Also Beautiful", rushlimbaugh.com/daily, November 20, 2015.

[16] https://en.wikipedia.org/wiki/Melania_Trump

[17] Donald J. Trump for President Campaign Slogan https://www.donaldjtrump.com

[18] DePaulo, Lisa (April 2007). "Ivanka Trump's Plan For Total World Domination". GQ Magazine.

[19] Gurley, George (January 29, 2007). "Trump Power". Marie Claire

[20] http://www.erictrumpfoundation.com/

[21] Meet Donald Trump's five children. Business Insider. Retrieved on October 30, 2015

[22] "Ivana Trump becomes U.S. citizen". Associated Press. May 27, 1988

[23] "IvanaTrump.com". IvanaTrump.com

[24] Barbara Walters Interview on ABC's 20/20 https://www.youtube.com/watch?v=FDiaNUoiB14

[25] "Donald Trump Ran for President in 2000 in Several Reform Party Primaries". Ballot Access News. Richard Wagner.

[26] "Trump in '04: 'I probably identify more as Democrat'". CNN. July 22, 2015.

[27] Haberman, Maggie (March 7, 2011).Trump tops Romney, Pawlenty. WNBC.

[28] Schoen, Douglas (February 21, 2011). "Obama Hits 50 Percent Approval Rating, According to New Newsweek/Daily Beast Poll". Newsweek / Daily Beast Company LLC.

[29] "Public Policy Polling" (PDF).

[30] "Donald Trump Places Sixth On Gallup's 'Most Admired' List". The Huffington Post, December 28, 2011.

[31] MacAskill, Ewen (May 16, 2011). "Donald Trump bows out of 2012 US presidential election race". The Guardian

[32] Milbank, Dana (February 13, 2011). "The Donald trumps the pols at CPAC". The Washington Post.

[33] "Donald Trump to address CPAC". Yahoo! News.

[34] Feely, Paul (February 27, 2015). "Trump won't renew 'Apprentice' so that he might focus on a presidential run". New Hampshire Union Leader.

[35] Evans, Kelly (April 19, 2011)."Trump: If President I Would Tariff China at 25%?. The Wall Street Journal.

[36] http://www.businessinsider.com/google-searches-map-donald-trump

[37] http://www.thenewsstar.com/story/news/politics/2014/09/14/endorsements-help-candidates/15637481/

[38] http://video.foxnews.com/v/4737305803001/scott-brown-explains-why-he-chose-to-endorse-donald-trump/?playlist_id=2114913880001#sp=show-clips

[39] Goode, Virgil (November 2, 2015). "Former Rep. Virgil Goode: Donald Trump For President, 'Only Candidate Truly Focused On' Immigration". Breitbart.

[40] Easley, Jonathan (August 21, 2015). "Trump Nears 100 Days on Top". The Hill.

[41] "Donald J. Trump Endorsed by Jeff DeWit, State Treasurer of Arizona". Blog.4president.org. January 20, 2016.

[42] "Donald J. Trump Endorsed by Jeff DeWit, State Treasurer of Arizona". Blog.4president.org. January 20, 2016.

[43] "Donald J. Trump Endorsed by Jeff DeWit, State Treasurer of Arizona". Blog.4president.org. January 20, 2016.

[44] Kiely, Kathy (August 21, 2015)."The Trump Bowl: Republican Front-Runner Packs 'Em In For Friday Night Rally". Bloomberg.

[45] "Donald J. Trump Files to be on the Ballot in Alabama". Blog.4president.org. November 5, 2015

[46] "Donald Trump Atlanta Rally". GAPundit. October 10, 2015.

[47] "Donald J. Trump Receives Endorsement of Iowa State Senator Brad Zaun". The Star-Ledger. October 15, 2015.

[48] The Moon Griffon Show, January 5, 2016

[49] "Robert Burns, Richard Ferdinando to endorse Donald Trump". WMUR. December 6, 2015.

[50] "The Trump Campaign Releases Initial List of 'Women for Trump' Coalition in New Hampshire". Democracy in Action. July 9, 2015.

[51] Ben Jacobs. "'This country's bankrupt': supporters keep Donald Trump in business". The Guardian.

[52] "Donald J. Trump Announces County Chairs in New Hampshire". Donald J Trump for President. May 21, 2015.

[53] "Donald J. Trump Announces the Formation of "Veterans for Trump" Coalition in New Hampshire". Democracy in Action. July 23, 2015.

[54] "Donald J. Trump Announces the Formation of "Veterans for Trump" Coalition in New Hampshire".Democracy in Action. July 23, 2015.

[55] "Donald J. Trump Endorsed by New Hampshire State Representative Stephen Stepanek". Donald J Trump for President. Retrieved July 17, 2015.

[56] "Donald J. Trump Announces the Formation of "Veterans for Trump" Coalition in New Hampshire". Democracy in Action. July 23, 2015.

[57] Epstein, Reid J. (June 16, 2015)."Donald Trump Vows to Disrupt Crowded GOP Presidential Race".*The Wall Street Journal*. Retrieved July 17,2015.

[58] "N.J. GOP lawmaker chooses Trump over Christie for 2016 prez race". The Star-Ledger. October 14, 2015

[59] "Donald J. Trump Receives Endorsements from #Oklahoma Leaders. #Trump2016 #MakeAmericaGreatAgain". Twitter. October 15, 2015

[60] ["Donald J. Trump Announces Joseph A. Trillo as Rhode Island Honorary Chairman". Blog.4president.org. January 13, 2016.]

[61] Rucker, Philip (January 25, 2016). "S.C. Republican who called Nikki Haley 'a raghead' to endorse Trump". The Washington Post.

[62] Andrew Shain (March 19, 2015). "2016 in SC: Donald Trump headlining Horry County GOP convention". The State

[63] "West Virginia Secretary of State, List of Candidates". January 21, 2016.

[64] http://www.cnn.com/2016/01/15/politics/donald-trump-pizza-ranch-retail-politics/index.html?sr=fbpol011516donald-trump-pizza-ranch-retail-politic0901PMStoryLink&linkId=20404644

[65] "Carl Icahn accepts Donald Trump's offer to be Treasury Secretary". Business Insider. August 8, 2015

[66] Kiyosaki, Robert (20 October 2015). "Why America Needs Donald Trump". Jetset Magazine. Retrieved 21 November 2015.

[67] "Donald Trump allies quietly seek money from rich, anonymous patrons". CNN. Retrieved 2015-09-12.

[68] "Donald Trump announces two new SC hires in presidential bid". The State. August 25, 2015.

[69] Maryalice Parks (September 25, 2015). "'Duck Dynasty' Star Willie Robertson Backs Trump, Saying 'I Do Like Me Some Trump'". ABC News.

[70] Maryalice Parks (September 25, 2015). "'Duck Dynasty' Star Willie Robertson Backs Trump, Saying 'I Do Like Me Some Trump'". ABC News.

[71] "Ivanka Trump touts dad's deal making in radio ad - CNNPolitics.com". CNN. Retrieved 2016-01-23

[72] "Dana White -- I'm Voting for Trump". TMZ. Retrieved December 11, 2015.

[73] "'Donald Trump is a hero': Italy's far-right leader". The Local. 2015-12-15.

[74] Nikolic, Ivana (2016-01-04). "Serbian Nationalist Leader Seselj Backs Donald Trump". Balkan Insight

[75] "Wilders: 'Hopelijk wordt Trump president'". FOK.nl (in Dutch). 2015-12-08.

[76] "Nationalist Pays For Radio Airtime and Robocalls to Promote Donald Trump - American Freedom Party". American Freedom Party.

[77] Ellefson, Lindsey (22 January 2016). "Donald Trump Gets Endorsed by National Black Republican Association". Mediaite.

[78] "New England Police Union Endorses Donald Trump". Retrieved 2015-12-10

[79] "Rent Is Too Damn High Party founder Jimmy McMillan endorses Donald Trump for president". January 29, 2016.

[80] https://www.facebook.com/DonaldTrump/?fref=ts

[81] https://www.youtube.com/watch?v=s8QR7BjSNv4

[82] https://www.youtube.com/watch?v=s8QR7BjSNv4

[83] Edwards-Levy, Ann (May 10, 2012). "Sarah Palin Endorses Ted Cruz For U.S. Senate In Texas". Yahoo!.

[84] http://www.hulu.com/watch/34465 From SNL Season 34 Episode 1 | Aired: 09/13/2008

[85] http://www.savingcountrymusic.com/destroying-the-dixie-chicks-ten-years-after/

[86] https://en.wikipedia.org/wiki/Dixie_Chicks

[87] https://www.youtube.com/watch?v=Ai0YOtzF2AA

[88] http://blogs.reuters.com/talesfromthetrail/2016/01/08/country-musician-loretta-lynn-to-trump-call-me/

[89] https://www.youtube.com/watch?v=yoqKdWY692k

90 Read more at http://dcwhispers.com/clint-eastwood-supports-donald-trump-others-anyone-of-them-better-than-what-weve-got/#sDprfzA1YxKcTvJh.99

91 http://www.msnbc.com/msnbc/willie-robertson-endorses-trump-one-week-after-his-dad-endorsed-cruz

92 http://www.huffingtonpost.com/entry/mike-tyson-endorses-donald-trump-2016_us_562e8853e4b00aa54a4aba46

93 http://transcripts.cnn.com/TRANSCRIPTS/1507/14/cnnt.01.html

94 http://www.foxnews.com/entertainment/2015/09/15/donald-trump-gets-coveted-gary-busey-endorsement-ahead-big-debate/

95 https://www.mrconservative.com/2015/10/65627-black-hollywood-star-risks-everything-to-endorse-trump-liberals-are-livid/

96 Rodham Endorsement http://www.businessinsider.com/donald-trump-celebrity-endorsements-2015-10

97 "How Pumping Iron Gave Birth to the Incredible Hulk". Arnold Body Building. Retrieved 5 April 2013.

98 https://www.youtube.com/watch?v=gDOdVqk-OC4

99 http://www.tmz.com/2015/08/29/hulk-hogan-wwe-is-my-family-no-hard-feelings-with-vince-mcmahon/

100 https://www.facebook.com/WestCoast2PACMakavelli/posts/10154013936969369:0

101 http://www.wnd.com/2015/07/give-trump-the-medal-of-freedom/#EWZSLvevtFc212K2.99

102 https://www.youtube.com/user/VenturaOffGrid

103 https://twitter.com/charliesheen/status/622575957770027009

104 https://twitter.com/charliesheen/status/636971482438959104?ref_src=twsrc%5Etfw

105 http://pagesix.com/2015/10/25/ivana-trump-campaigns-for-donald/

106 http://www.tmz.com/2015/12/14/herschel-walker-donald-trump-president/

107 http://www.breitbart.com/sports/2016/01/27/iowa-football-players-rally-for-trump/

108 http://chicago.suntimes.com/sports/7/71/942562/4-downs-ditka-like-donald-trump

[109] Read more: http://www.tmz.com/2015/06/16/terrell-owens-endorsing-donald-trump-president-youre-hired-apprentice/#ixzz3yI6E6KPG

[110] https://www.youtube.com/watch?v=Hal4LmPRB9I

[111] http://www.nydailynews.com/news/politics/rapper-chingy-announces-donald-trump-endorsement-article-1.2506248

[112] http://www.breitbart.com/big-hollywood/2015/11/30/robert-davi-donald-trump-is-the-john-wayne-of-politics/

[113] http://www.rollingstone.com/music/news/kid-rock-im-digging-donald-trump-20160201

[114] https://www.washingtonpost.com/news/post-politics/wp/2016/01/26/evangelical-leader-jerry-falwell-jr-endorses-trump/

[115] http://www.wnd.com/2015/12/top-conservative-trump-is-last-hope-for-america/

[116] http://www.thepoliticalinsider.com/franklin-graham-makes-a-huge-announcement-about-donald-trump/

[117] https://www.facebook.com/FranklinGraham/posts/966608693395312

[118] Wes Vernon (June 21, 2015). "Book Review: 'Adios America: The Left's Plan to Turn Our Country into a Third World Hellhole'". The Washington Times

[119] https://www.youtube.com/watch?v=cJ8du4kxUUQ

[120] http://www.newsmax.com/Headline/Michael-Savage-Donald-Trump-winston-churchill-supports/2015/07/29/id/659542/#ixzz3yJsAi8CE

[121] https://www.youtube.com/watch?v=es5SnPYkGiA

[122] http://www.washingtontimes.com/news/2015/dec/16/donald-trump-teams-up-with-joe-arpaio-in-mesa-ariz/?page=all#pagebreak

[123] http://www.breitbart.com/big-government/2016/01/26/report-maricopa-county-sheriff-arpaio-to-endorse-donald-trump/

[124] Read more: http://www.tmz.com/2015/12/11/dana-white-donald-trump-vote-president/#ixzz3yMu5g8rt

[125] http://thehill.com/blogs/ballot-box/presidential-races/264988-bill-clinton-rape-accuser-hillary-tried-to-silence-me

[126] http://thehill.com/blogs/in-the-know/in-the-know/268100-paula-jones-i-like-trump

127 https://www.noagendaplayer.com/listen/741/1-28-18
128

https://www.reddit.com/r/SquaredCircle/comments/43lj1p/im_wwe_hal
l_of_famer_the_million_dollar_man_ted/czj5q09
129 http://baesic.net/minutemanproject/minuteman-project-leader-
endorses-donald-trump-for-president-suggests-cruz-run-as-vp/
130 https://www.youtube.com/watch?v=0QkJxwWxqZI
131 http://personalliberty.com/only-donald-trump-can-beat-ruthless-
hillary-heres-why/
132 http://www.breitbart.com/tech/2016/01/15/milo-yiannopoulos-
trump-will-make-america-fabulous-again/
133 https://www.youtube.com/watch?v=J0nklA02iVg&feature=em-
lbrm
134

https://www.facebook.com/TrumpGeorgia/posts/1543622592597660?n
otif_t=notify_me_page
135 http://money.cnn.com/2015/03/20/news/economy/millennials-
jobs-college/
136 http://reason.com/assets/db/2014-millennials-report.pdf
137 http://www.newsmax.com/TheWire/donald-trump-quotes-2016-
race/2016/02/09/id/713408/
138 http://www.cbsnews.com/news/donald-trump-is-running-for-
president-in-2016/
139 http://www.cbsnews.com/news/donald-trump-is-running-for-
president-in-2016/
140 http://www.cbsnews.com/news/donald-trump-is-running-for-
president-in-2016/
141 http://www.cnn.com/2015/06/28/politics/donald-trump-
immigration-gay-marriage-2016/index.html
142 http://www.cnn.com/2016/02/06/politics/donald-trump-new-
hampshire-drug-epidemic/
143 http://www.breitbart.com/big-government/2015/09/09/trump-
israel-will-not-survive-with-iran-nuclear-deal-in-place/
144 http://www.nbcnews.com/politics/2016-election/south-carolina-
rally-trump-defiant-steadfast-muslim-ban-n475951

145 http://www.telegraph.co.uk/news/worldnews/donald-trump/12039781/Donald-Trump-areas-of-London-so-radicalised-police-fear-for-their-lives.html

146 http://www.nationalreview.com/article/428719/kill-terrorists-families-gangsta-trump

147 http://www.telegraph.co.uk/news/worldnews/northamerica/usa/120109 28/Donald-Trump-repeats-discredited-claims-that-US-Muslims-celebrated-911-attacks.html

148 http://news.yahoo.com/ten-quotes-republican-debate-083909819.html

149 http://talkingpointsmemo.com/livewire/donald-trump-ben-carson-pathological-child-molester

150 http://www.c-span.org/video/?c4545110/donald-trump-john-mccain-hes-war-hero-captured-like-people-werent-captured

151 http://www.huffingtonpost.com/entry/donald-trump-gay-marriage_us_55df3412e4b029b3f1b1d228

152 http://www.cbsnews.com/news/donald-trump-60-minutes-scott-pelley/

153 http://nymag.com/daily/intelligencer/2016/01/donald-trump-skip-fox-news-debate.html

154 http://www.newsmax.com/Headline/fox-trump-debate-lowest/2016/01/29/id/711838/   ©2016 Thomson/Reuters

155 http://www.breitbart.com/big-government/2016/01/28/live-updates-donald-trumps-veteran-fundraiser/

156 http://www.realclearpolitics.com/epolls/2016/president/ia/iowa_republi can_presidential_caucus-3194.html

157 http://www.breitbart.com/big-government/2016/02/01/iowa/

158 http://www.msnbc.com/msnbc/carson-other-campaigns-sabotaged-us-dirty-tricks

159 http://www.foxbusiness.com/features/2016/02/02/ben-carson-cruzs-apology-needs-accountability.html

160 http://www.radioiowa.com/2016/02/04/branstad-says-cruz-employed-unethical-and-unfair-tactics-monday-night/

161 http://www.newsmax.com/TheWire/donald-trump-iowa-caucus-ted-cruz/2016/02/02/id/712359/

162 http://www.washingtonexaminer.com/byron-york-gop-fear-and-loathing-in-new-hampshire/article/2581329

163 http://www.harperpolling.com/polls/new-hampshire-republican-presidential-primary-poll

164 http://www.whdh.com/story/31126831/hiller-instinct-7newsumass-lowell-new-hampshire-tracking-poll-day-3

165 http://www.breitbart.com/big-government/2016/02/02/report-donald-trump-nominated-for-noble-peace-prize-peace-through-strength-ideology/

www.ingramcontent.com/pod-product-compliance
Lightning Source LLC
Chambersburg PA
CBHW062124280526
45788CB00001B/45